9/21

D1008796

# Winning the
# Brain Game

# Winning the
# Brain Game

### FIXING THE 7 FATAL
### FLAWS OF THINKING

## MATTHEW E. MAY

New York   Chicago   San Francisco   Athens   London   Madrid
Mexico City   Milan   New Delhi   Singapore   Sydney   Toronto

1 2 3 4 5 6 7 8 9 0    DOC    19 18 17 16

ISBN        978-1-259-64239-5
MHID        1-259-64239-9

e-ISBN    978-1-259-64240-1
e-MHID    1-259-64240-2

**Library of Congress Cataloging-in-Publication Data**

May, Matthew E.
Winning the brain game : fixing the 7 fatal flaws of thinking / Matthew E.
   May.
New York : McGraw-Hill, 2016.
LCCN 2015051017| ISBN 9781259642395 (alk. paper) | ISBN 1259642399
   (alk. paper)
LCSH: Thought and thinking. | Reasoning. | Decision making. | Mind and
   body.
LCC BF441 .M3495 2016 | DDC 153.4/2--dc23 LC record available at
   http://lccn.loc.gov/2015051017

McGraw-Hill Education books are available at special quantity discounts to use as premiums and sales promotions or for use in corporate training programs. To contact a representative, please visit the Contact Us pages at www.mhprofessional.com.

Cover design by Joanne Lee.

A MANTRA

*What appears to be the problem, isn't.*
*What appears to be the solution, isn't.*
*What appears to be impossible, isn't.*
**—THE ELEGANT SOLUTION**

# CONTENTS

## PART ONE
## Misleading

## PART TWO
## Mediocre

## PART THREE
## Mindless

# ACKNOWLEDGMENTS

This book almost wasn't. Undoubtedly due to one or more flaws in my thinking, I had somehow convinced myself that most of the world no longer had the time or interest in reading books, and that the volume of noise in the form of information was already so overwhelming to most people that another book would only speed the saturation level. It was self-censorsing at its finest, and it took a good bit of poking and prodding from my wise advocate and agent John Willig to convince me I was wrong, and to give it another go. He had help from Knox Huston, my terrific editor from McGraw-Hill. I am grateful to them both for getting me to practice what I preach, to look at things from another perspective, and to produce an elegant solution. I am really proud of this little book, and I think it may indeed be my best work. For the first time in a decade of authorship, I have a book that has broad appeal and universal applicability, regardless of one's walk in life. That's cool. Thank you, gentlemen.

As to the content of the book itself, I have several thinking partners I would like to thank, not simply for lending me their expertise and advice in the production of this book, but for their counsel and mentorship over the past several years. I am quite fortunate to have as distant colleagues some of the world's most noteworthy thought leaders, including those whose wisdom figures centrally in *Winning the Brain Game*.

For helping me distill and decode matters of neuroscience and the clear distinction between the mind and the brain, I have Dr. Jeffrey Schwartz to thank. Jeff is a master at helping people unlock their brains, and has been a colleague and advisor to me for many years.

For helping me understand the nuances of revealing hidden assumptions and teaching me techniques to engage what he refers to as "the opposable mind," I have the brilliant Roger Martin, dean emeritus of The Rotman School and Thinkers50 leader, to thank. For well over a half decade, Roger has been a mentor and collaborator.

On matters of professional curiosity, constant experimentation, and serious play, I have the relentless provocateur Michael Schrage of MIT to thank. Just when you think you know something, Michael has the uncanny ability to inject the very question that lets you know you don't.

Finally, I wish to thank the ever mindful Ellen Langer for graciously spending a bit of her time with me and sharing a story that I had not heard or seen written before.

If you enjoy *Winning the Brain Game*, it is because I had these individuals to help me bring it to life.

# Mind Over Matter

*You have to learn the rules of the game. And then you have to play better than anyone else.*

**—ALBERT EINSTEIN**

What would you do if someone handed you a difficult problem to solve right now? Would you don your thinking cap, look up to the right, touch your chin, knit your brow, shrug your shoulders, then throw your hands up in the air after a few minutes, declaring the problem to be impossible to solve? Would you search your memory banks for how you or someone solved a similar problem in the past and, coming up empty-handed, search Google to see if and how others might have solved it? Would you immediately and instinctively launch into a concerted effort to brainstorm top-of-mind solutions in a shotgun fashion, hoping that some mental spaghetti might stick to the wall? Would you smile, surrender, confess to having no clue, ask for the solution, then upon hearing it, slap your forehead and cry, "Of course! Why didn't I think of that?" Would you experience a sudden creative insight, see the solution immediately, but then second-guess yourself, unconsciously judging your solution to be too simplistic and too obvious to be a good one, and voluntarily kill a great idea?

Hard for me to say, because I don't know you. But the odds of you doing something very similar are very good. In fact, you will probably do it sometime today. Meanwhile, that nasty problem goes unsolved.

But it doesn't have to be that way.

I intended this book to be a mindful guide—complete with a super-curated set of battle-tested tools—for using our minds to win the games our brains are hardwired to play on us, the patterns of tricks that while effective in handling routine problems and quick-fix situations, become traps when we need to invoke our best thinking. This struggle of mind over matter *is* the brain game. (See what I did there? I made a distinction between the mind and the brain. Keep that in mind as you read on.)

I stumbled on these patterns over 10 years ago in my role as a professional facilitator, working with Toyota's U.S.-based corporate university. We were using a few different thought challenges, based on real business stories, as icebreakers for a course called Principled Problem-Solving. We were surprised first by how many people failed to solve the challenges, second by the redundancy in the solutions offered up, and third, but most importantly, by the repetitive nature of thinking and behavior patterns.

I left my gig with Toyota after spending eight years with them, but kept using similar, real-world thought challenges in workshops, seminars, and speaking engagements all over the world. No matter where I went or to whom I gave the problems, the results were eerily similar. Over 100,000 people have now gone through these exercises with me, and in spite of all that has been discovered and written about the brain and the mind during the past three decades, I continue to observe these patterns. The evidence I've collected is overwhelming, and points to seven readily observable behaviors, which I call fatal flaws of thinking . . . mental glitches, if you will, that if left unchecked may just leave us wondering why our deepest problems never get solved.

I confess that I never set out to conduct a long-term study, for I am neither scientist nor scholar. I'm far better at applying all those wonderful scientific discoveries and putting into practice what scholars propose in theoretical frameworks, to see whether what they say *should* work actually *does* in the real world. In that way, I'm much more like the jeweler seeking to fix a stuck gear in a wristwatch than the philosopher pontificating on a theory of time.

When it comes to the frontiers of consciousness and cognition, I have neither the inclination nor intelligence to study or explain in any real depth the vastly complex inner workings of our grey matter. I can't even pronounce most parts of the brain cited in books and articles. Furthermore, that territory is quite well-traversed, from the work of early-twentieth-century Gestalt psychologists to modern day fMRI-wielding cognitive neuroscientists, and widely available in myriad other books and articles. It is best for all concerned that I simply summon and synthesize all that amazing insight and point it toward my real worry, which is how to master our greatest asset—our mind—to our best advantage in winning the brain game. (Catch that? I did it again.)

Nor do I wish to delve deeply into the rather broad and nebulous space we call creativity, and creative problem solving. I'm far more interested in removing the obstacles that may be blocking one's naturally creative mind from more regularly producing the brilliance I know it's capable of. In that sense, this book is more like a repair manual that helps your mind fix the seven fatal thinking flaws your brain commits. (Third time!) If I could change the world in one single way, that would be it. It's the great ambition of this little book, and if Malcolm Gladwell is correct in asserting that little things can make a big difference, the odds may just tip in my favor.

The question, of course, is how to effect such a tip? First, by exposing these flaws to the widest audience possible. I'll need your help to do that. Second, by revealing a tad of the mechanics behind why they are so prevalent. I'm fortunate to have spent time with some of the foremost psychologists and neuroscientists, and this much I know from working with them: there is a significant distinction between the brain and the mind. The brain is passive hardware, absorbing experience, and the mind is active software, directing our attention. But not just any software—it's intelligent software capable of rewiring the hardware. I could not have said that with confidence a few decades ago, but modern science is a wonderful thing.

The third and final way is by introducing you to the seven "fixes"—tools and techniques that I as well as others have developed, and which through my work I have found to be among the most effective and practical ways to not only neutralize the fatal flaws of thinking, but also forge new neural connections in the brain.

I will ask you to keep a simple mantra in mind at all times:

What appears to be the problem, isn't.
What appears to be the solution, isn't.
What appears to be impossible, isn't.

This book represents a short and user-friendly distillation of everything I've learned in my three decades of facilitating and coaching individuals and teams as they pursue their most important challenges. In an effort to continuously improve my own and others' mental capability, I've watched tens of thousands of people, incorporated the work of highly regarded scientists, scholars, and strategists, experimented with hundreds of both original and borrowed techniques, and made hundreds of mistakes. My aim is to spare you from having to do all that on your own. It is a book that is meant not simply to be read, but to be used. Again and again. Not a bad deal for 20 bucks.

While I cannot grant you the gift of flawless thinking, it is indeed the thought that counts.

INTRODUCTION

# 7 Fatal Flaws

*We cannot solve our problems with the same thinking
we used when we created them.*

**—ALBERT EINSTEIN**

t's 2005. I am seated in a corporate conference
room on the top floor of an eight-story building in southern California, surrounded by 12
highly skilled bomb technicians from the Los Angeles Police
Department who have been hand-picked and gathered to
address a complex challenge regarding new methods and
approaches needed to respond to bomb calls in the new
age of everyday terrorism. They received their training at
the same Kentucky facility that trains all bomb technicians
in the United States, regardless of military or paramilitary
branch.

The problem is as wicked as a problem could possibly
be: how to handle fluid, potentially catastrophic situations
involving highly lethal improvised explosive devices (IEDs)
capable of massive devastation and death in public places.

The current strategy isn't working as well as they need it
to, because a new breed of terrorism has entered the mix, one
that is unpredictable, constantly changing, operates an essentially leaderless organization, defies all conventional warfare,

logic, and rationality, and has no qualms about taking the lives of civilians . . . or their own lives, for that matter.

I am excited to have been chosen to be the facilitator over the course of the next two days, at the end of which they will present their solution to LAPD's counterterrorism senior command staff. I am also as apprehensive as I've ever been, with any team, anywhere, in any setting.

These are the most highly paid officers in the entire department, the guys and gals who have to cut the right wire, so to speak. It's a job that requires quick thinking, quick reads, quick decisions, and quick action—all under enormous pressure in a situation that presents them with something they've never seen before. They often must improvise in a split second. They do not have time in the field to think deeply.

Above all, they are men and women of action. Sitting in a brainstorming session with some civilian who possesses absolutely no experience or expertise in doing their incredibly challenging job isn't exactly their cup of tea. They didn't volunteer to be here. They'd rather be out chasing bad guys and protecting the world from the evil crazies. The fully armed officer to my left takes off his gun belt and riot stick, then leans over to whisper, "I'm only here because I was ordered." This doesn't help my level of apprehension. I am unarmed.

There's a good bit of discomfort, skepticism, and tension in the air. So while I have no explosives training, I do need to defuse the situation just a bit. I certainly have no authority over them, but I do "own" the process. I need to not only establish some rules of engagement, but do so in way that opens minds and encourages divergent thinking, because that's what's needed here. Go-go "Git 'er done" thinking won't cut it.

By way of introduction, I ask the good problem-solvers to raise their hand. Every hand goes up. No surprises there, bombs are problems, and problem-solving is the air they breathe. I tell them to keep their hands held high, which they do with surprising obedience. I continue the query, by asking those who consider themselves great learners to now raise their other hand. Same result, all hands up. Twelve LAPD officers with both arms up in the air. I can't resist: "Do I ever wish I had a camera right now." Grins, groans, eyerolls, snickers. Then, I ask the true innovators to keep their hands up. Every hand down. No takers. None.

I didn't ask that question to destroy confidence, but to change the frame. I make the point that as a practical matter, innovation, problem-solving, and true learning—the kind where new knowledge is actually created by the learner— employ the same iterative process: questioning, framing, hypothesizing, ideating, testing, reflecting. So, I've essentially now dubbed them innovators.

The ice may be melting, but it's not quite broken. Because they're accustomed to working closely with a partner, I split the group into six pairs and give them a quick thought challenge to tackle, one based on a real problem and involving something they're fairly familiar with—compliance—but one that is much simpler than any problem they will ever face on the job.

My hypothesis is that the LAPD bomb techs will do what everyone else I had ever seen work on this kind of challenge had done, in all the same ways, and in all probability fail to solve the problem.

## THOUGHT CHALLENGE*

Imagine that you own a luxury health club. As part of the membership perks, each of the 40 shower stalls—20 men's and 20 women's—is stocked with a bottle of very expensive ($50), salon-only shampoo, which is only available in beauty supply retail stores to licensed hair stylists. The customers love it and rave about this particular perk. Unfortunately, bottles disappear from the showers all the time. In fact, the theft rate is 33 percent, presenting a costly situation, not to mention a bad experience for members reaching for the shampoo, only to find the bottle gone. Your staff must constantly resolve complaints among your "honest" members. You've tried a number of things to solve the problem: reminders, penalties, and incentives to try and reduce theft, but nothing so far has worked. The front desk even sells the bottles at a very slim profit margin.

You decide to ask your employees, all of whom are hourly, to help solve the problem, and give them several nonnegotiable conditions: the solution must completely eliminate theft; it cannot involve discontinuing or limiting the current shampoo offering in any way (one full-size bottle of the current brand per stall must not change); any solution must be of extremely low, and preferably no, cost (pennies per stall, at most); there can be no additional burden on the member; and the solution must be easy to implement, without disrupting the normal operation of the club.

---

* This problem is based on a Los Angeles-area health club. I turned the story into a thought challenge.

You tell your employees that they are free to be as innovative as they wish and do anything they want, as long as all conditions are met.

I reiterate to the bomb tech team that they are free to be as innovative as they wish, come up with any solution they wish, be as wild and crazy as they wish, but that their idea will be peer-graded by the rest of the room on the basis of how well their solution meets *all* of the conditions, while violating none. And because working under time pressure is part of their job, I give them just five minutes to come up with their best idea. I challenge them to match their problem-solving chops with those of the part-time health club employees, who in fact solved the problem elegantly. I put a little skin in the game and tell them that the team that comes up with the best idea gets a special gift. It's now a friendly competition.

I'd been using another version of this exercise* in a creative problem-solving seminar at the University of Toyota, and my observations of several hundred participants over the course of several months had begun to reveal some interesting patterns. I liked these types of challenges for several reasons. First, because they are based on very real business problems and, as mentioned, are far less complex than everyday work-related problems. Second, because these sorts of conundrums catch people doing many if not all of the things that prevent them from seeing the solution that achieves the maximum effect with the minimum means. I have for years used this as the simple definition of an *elegant solution*.

---

* I will share another version of the exercise with you later in the book.

## THE ELEGANT SOLUTION

One that achieves the maximum effect with minimum means.

Try your hand at solving this thought exercise. Put this book down and let your mind play with the possibilities. I'll even double your resources: you have 10 minutes. Enlist the help of someone else if you like—some people prefer to collaborate. Jot down all your ideas, select the best one, and then we'll continue.

Seriously, try it. I'll wait. The rest of the book will be more meaningful if you do.

Back? How did it go? Do you think you came up with the elegant solution? If you're like 95 percent of the people I give this kind of problem to, including the LAPD bomb techs, you undoubtedly came up with several ideas.

Here are the most frequently given solutions:

- keep bottles at the front desk to check in and out
- hire a locker room attendant to check them in and out
- put travel-size bottles in the stalls
- install cameras
- loyalty program offering a free bottle for keeping a clean record
- install lockable pump-top dispensers in each stall
- have a gym bag-checker at the exit
- discontinue the shampoo in the stalls
- charge a separate fee for shampoo
- sell the shampoo at cost

- "most wanted list": pictures and names of offenders
- chain the bottles somehow to the wall
- put the shampoo in unmarked bottles
- install "do not remove shampoo" signs in stalls
- give out free sample-size bottles at the front desk
- hire shower security guards
- puncture the side of the bottle near the top
- install radio-frequency identification (RFID)
- consider loss due to theft a cost of doing business
- keep the bottles near empty at all times

Unfortunately, all of these solutions violate one or more of the conditions imposed—some more than others, of course—and none of them represent the rather elegant solution produced by the health club employees, which I will get to in a bit.

## THE SEVEN FLAWS & FIXES

Every time I watch folks wrestle with this challenge, I'm constantly amazed at how people so consistently fall victim to the same patterned thinking traps and exhibit the same kinds of behaviors over and over again. I was not disappointed as I watched the bomb techs work.

The scientific community has a whole host of sophisticated labels and pet names for these behaviors, as well as a long laundry list of other patterns, but let me simplify things a bit: they are fatal thinking flaws. There are seven of them. Each carries with it the potential to kill a great idea, and prevent an elegant solution from ever seeing the light of day.

That there happen to be seven is purely coincidence!

## 1. Leaping

When I watched the LAPD bomb techs work on the problem, they immediately began offering up solutions in rapid-fire fashion. They spent nearly all their time doing one thing: brainstorming. Or as designerly types call it, ideating. (Horrible word. Hate it.) What struck me as curious was that they invested little if any time doing what they were all actually trained very well to to do: first gather the facts, then synthesize them into a theory of the crime and the motive behind it, before ever trying to solve it. Sherlock Holmes would've been disappointed, having advised Watson in no uncertain terms, "It is a capital mistake to theorize before one has facts. Insensibly one begins to twist facts to suit theories instead of theories to suit facts." In real terms, they bypassed entirely any discussion of why people were stealing the shampoo.

Moreover, the conditions of the challenge are generally ignored. I have observed that it appears to be easier, or at least more common, for people to think "outside the box" than inside it; and that is not necessarily a good thing.

Immediately and instinctively leaping to solutions in a sort of mental knee jerk almost never leads to an elegant solution to an unfamiliar, complex problem, because not enough time is devoted to framing the issue properly. In the thought exercise, I listed facts and constraints in a slightly disguised attempt to paint a picture of the desired future. I did not, however, explicitly frame the problem. I wanted to leave that to the LAPD bomb techs, and to you.

Perhaps you thought you were solving the problem of dishonesty, which is one way to frame the challenge. But it is not the only way, nor is it the best or most useful way, because your chances of alchemically transforming dishonesty to honesty in the context of petty theft are, well, nil. There is an art to framing and reframing problems, and part of the art is in the timing. The fix for the Leaping flaw is generating multiple ways to frame the problem. In other words, instead of coming up with answers right away, you come up with questions right away. It's called *Framestorming*.

In this case, figuring out why people are stealing the shampoo is key. Dishonesty is indeed one cause, but one too abstract to correct. There are others, including accessibility to a highly desirable item. The bottle of shampoo is too tempting, at least for a third of the health club's patrons. Once you understand that, you can frame the problem to focus on the question of how to make it utterly undesirable to remove the bottle of shampoo, without incurring cost or burden to anyone. Remove the temptation, eliminate theft entirely.

Framing a problem properly has everything to do with whether it gets solved elegantly.

## 2. Fixation

Fixation is an umbrella term for our general mental rigidity and linear thinking—our go-to mindsets, blind spots, paradigms, schemas, biases, mental maps, and models—that make it easier for us to make it through the day, but harder for us to flex and shift our perception. The term itself comes from what psychologists call "functional fixedness." Our brains are amazing pattern machines: making, recognizing, and acting on patterns developed from our experiences and grooved over time. Following those grooves makes us ever so efficient as we go about our day. The challenge is this: if left to its own devices, the brain locks in on patterns, and it's difficult to escape the gravitational pull of embedded memory in order to see things in an altogether new light. In other words, those deep grooves make it tough to go off-road and, as the Apple tagline goes, think different.

Fixation and Leaping are interconnected . . . two sides of the same coin. If you spend a bit more time framing the problem properly, you can often avoid getting mentally stuck in gear. In the shampoo bottle challenge, your brain may have blocked any notion of decomposing the image of the bottle itself: bottle with top, one unit, inseparable.

The health club's elegant solution? Remove the tops of the shampoo bottles. Problem solved. No one wanted to put a topless bottle of shampoo in their gym bag!

If you're thinking that this solution will irk the 67 percent of the patrons who weren't stealing shampoo, well, that's just your Fixation flaw speaking. The cure for Fixation is what I call *inversion*, and captures the essence of several creative thinking techniques used by designers and artists to radically shift their thinking from the current reality of how things are in order to pursue the possibility of how they could be: Steve Jobs was known for his "reality distortion field"; Stanford engineering professor Robert Sutton often refers to *vuja de*, which is the opposite of *deja vu**; his Stanford colleague and creativity professor Tina Seelig suggests that to spur new thinking we take the current conditions of the situation and think of the polar opposites; TED Ideas editor Helen Walters argues that we should regularly "flip orthodoxy."

---

* If *deja vu* is the feeling that a certain event has happened before, *vuja de* is the direct opposite . . . an event or situation that should be familiar is suddenly very different. The late comedian George Carlin jokingly coined the term, describing it as "the strange feeling that, somehow, none of this has ever happened before." https://youtu.be/B7LBSDQ14eA

## 3. Overthinking

On the other end of the thinking spectrum from Leaping is Overthinking, which can be thought of as our knack for creating problems that weren't even there in the first place. Overthinking is a rather deep bucket filled with a host of variations on a theme: overanalyzing, overplanning, and generally complicating matters by adding unnecessary complexity and cost. In looking at the list of most common theft-prevention solutions, notice that many require the addition of resources of some kind: manpower, money, material. Most of them not only violate the conditions of the challenge, but are completely impractical. We often ignore the most important constraints of a given problem, which blocks the discovery of a more elegant solution.

Why *do* we overthink, overanalyze, and complicate matters? Why *do* we add cost and complexity? Most interestingly, why do we all do it so naturally, intuitively, and, perhaps most disturbingly, so consistently?

Part of the answer is that we're hardwired that way. Through eons of evolution, our brains are designed to drive hoarding, storing, accumulating, collecting-type behavior. We are by nature "do more/add on" types. When it comes to problem-solving, this instinct translates into adding complexity and cost as a first course of action, especially when we recognize the problem as being a complex one requiring a deeper level of thinking, analysis, and planning. "I can solve the problem, but it's going to take more resources" is the oft-heard refrain. But it doesn't necessarily take genius to spend resources . . . it does, though, to work within the resource constraints you're given. What cost and complexity did you add in trying to solve the thought problems?

Another part of the answer is a simple lack of a reliable approach that enables us to grapple with uncertainty, risk, external forces beyond our control, and rapidly changing circumstances that eschew any sort of traditional planning. We've lost the required childlike learning and experimenting capability needed to make innovative problem-solving simpler, safer, and speedier. MIT's master of business experimentation Michael Schrage calls that capability "serious play," and puts it this way: "Innovation too often is too slow, too expensive, too complicated, too risky, too rigid, too dull, too little, and too late."[1] Schrage doesn't even like the word "idea" and prefers to couch all challenge-chasing efforts in terms of "simple, fast, and frugal" tests meant to reveal the validity of a concept.

He's right. Until any concept is raised to the level of reality, it is merely a guess, or set of guesses, in need of testing. The simple fix for Overthinking is *Prototesting*, a combination of prototyping and testing. From a back-of-the-napkin sketch to a first draft to a minimally functional mockup to technical A/B testing to the reverse engineering of a set of strategic choices, Prototesting enables us to tangibly tease out the mental leaps of faith made in crafting any kind of solution and run a simple test quickly and cheaply in order to learn. Prototesting lends proof of concept, with the intent being to prove an initial concept is worth developing further.

## 4. Satisficing

People favor action and implementation over nearly all else, and certainly over incubation. By nature we *satisfice*, a term combining satisfy and suffice, and coined by Nobel laureate

Herbert Simon in his 1957 book *Models of Man*. We glom on to what's easy and obvious and stop looking for the best or optimal solution, the one that resolves the problem within the given goals and constraints. We over-compromise and suboptimize, accepting the halfway solution and relying on our ability to push it forward. Unfortunately, when it comes to complex problems, that usually amounts to a rather Herculean but useless effort akin to pushing water uphill. We fool ourselves into thinking "good enough is," thereby creating something that demands massive work in order to succeed. By thinking less, we end up working more.

Breakthrough thinking demands something to break through. Generally, it's the space between conflicting goals, causing creative tension. With the shampoo example, I deliberately set goals in conflict under a short time frame to force a creative tension in your mind to raise awareness of what your brain is doing.

Did you refuse to make trade-offs, refuse to compromise on the criteria, or did you simply pick a solution at the 10-minute mark and rationalize why it would work?

As Rotman School professor and renowned business strategist Roger Martin tells us, "By putting in the necessary thinking work and refusing to accept the unattractive trade-offs, we can unleash our ability to build new and better models and create value for the world."[2] At the heart of Martin's integrative thinking methodology is a synthetic process that calls up what he terms the *opposable mind*, which merges the very best parts of two opposing but satisficing solutions in an elegant mash-up that defeats the tendency to satisfice and settle for anything less than the best solution.

The fix for Satisficing is thus: *Synthesis*.

## 5. Downgrading

Downgrading is the close cousin of satisficing, with a twist: a formal downward or backward revision of the goal or situation, often resulting in wholesale disengagement from the challenge. It comes in a few basic flavors. First, there's the twisting and sifting of facts to suit our solution, arrived at by Leaping or Fixation. Second, there is the "revised estimate." The result is the same: we fall short of the optimal or ideal solution, pick one that gets us most of the way there, then sell the upside and downplay the downside.

Basically, we commit what amounts to preemptive surrender, which in a perverse way enables us to do what we really want to do, which is to declare victory. We do it all the time, because no one wants to feel like they didn't succeed. It's not very resourceful, creative, or heroic.

But here's the thing: you can't win a football game by aiming for the 97-yard line. You can't score a run in baseball by only making it to third base. You can't reach Mars by shooting for the moon. You can't . . . well, you get the drift.

Studies of brainstorming sessions reveal that idea generation generally stalls after about 20 minutes. At that point most groups stop and turn their attention to evaluating their ideas. However, the research shows that teams with the best ideas don't stop there. Rather, they embrace the psychological barrier and push through the stall zone, somehow resetting their minds to opening up new channels of widely divergent thinking.

The fix for Downgrading is *Jumpstarting*, defined just as it is in the dictionary: starting a stalled vehicle whose battery is drained by connecting it to another source of power. Jumpstarting redoubles your focus on both your will and your way, the two elements needed to attain any well-set goal, to give yourself a boot in the brain in lieu of disengaging or abandoning the challenge entirely. Jumpstarting combines simple techniques that not only have recent studies shown to be quite effective for pushing past the surrender mark, but that I know to work in well in the field.

In considering the shampoo problem, did you think: 0 percent theft is impossible, throw up your hands and simply give up, turning the pages until you found the solution somewhere in the narrative? If you did, I bet the teacher caught you peeking at your neighbor's answers on that third-grade math quiz in elementary school.

I watched the bomb techs do the equivalent. They ran out of obvious ideas well before the five-minute mark, and immediately began looking at the other pairs around the room, looking for answers. Interestingly, even when a stolen glance yielded an idea they hadn't thought of, they would wrinkle their nose or shrug their shoulders, dismissing it out of hand.

This brings up the final two flaws, which deal with the outright rejection of ideas. There is a nuanced difference between rejecting ideas of others and rejecting ideas of our own, so I will treat them separately.

## 6. Not Invented Here (NIH)

NIH is a well known acronym in management literature* for "Not Invented Here" syndrome, defined as an automatic negative perception of, and visceral aversion to, concepts and solutions developed somewhere else, somewhere external to

---

* In a database search of scholarly papers, I found over 600 journal articles referring to NIH syndrome.

the individual or team, often resulting in an unnecessary reinvention of the wheel. It means, "If I/we didn't come up with it, I/we won't consider it," and "I/we can do anything you/they can do, better." We don't trust other people's solutions. While there may be a basis in neuroscience related to triggering our threat response, our expression of it is always the same: shutting out another person's or group's idea immediately and without due consideration merely because *they* came up with it. The next time you're in the lobby waiting for the elevator to go up to your office or hotel room, count how many people hit the up button even though they can see that you've already pushed it. That's NIH.

How much time did you spend pondering why previous solutions didn't work? I'll bet almost none. The LAPD bomb techs sure didn't. The impulse to do something, anything, and fast, leads us to focus on execution, and as a result we ignore the facts. In laying out the thought exercise, I specifically said that reminders, incentives, and penalties had not worked in the past. Yet it never fails: in every session in which I use this kind of thought exercise, I'm given some form of at least one of those. Go back a few pages and see how many of the popular ideas are really just another form of what hadn't worked in the past . . . reminders, incentives, penalties. Perhaps you caught yourself thinking, *they didn't do it right*, which is acceptable if you intend to focus on learning why those previous attempts failed, because doing so would eventually lead you to reframing the problem. But simply pushing your version of the same idea just because those other attempts didn't originate with you is harmful NIH.

As Walter Isaacson pointed out in his biography of the late Steve Jobs, most people know Apple took the graphic user interface from Xerox, an act "sometimes described as one of the biggest heists in the chronicles of industry." According to Isaacson, Jobs was proud of it, and said: "Picasso had a saying—'good artists copy, great artists steal'—and we have always been shameless about stealing great ideas. "

And therein lies the fix for NIH. Instead of calling it stealing, however, I will simply steal the phrase Procter & Gamble's open innovation program—Connect & Develop—coined when in 2000 newly appointed CEO A. G. Lafley decreed that fully 50 percent of the company's innovations must come from outside the organization: *Proudly Found Elsewhere (PFE)*. Implementing a PFE strategy is quite literally an opening of the mind to let in, leverage, and recycle the ideas and solutions of others.

## 7. Self-Censoring

When we reject, deny, stifle, squelch, strike, silence, and otherwise put *ideas of our own* to death, sometimes even before they're born, it is an act of Self-Censoring. I believe Self-Censoring is the deadliest of the fatal flaws, because in my admittedly subjective opinion, any voluntary shutdown of the imagination is an act of mindlessness, the long-term effects of which eventually kill off our natural curiosity and creativity. Like NIH, Self-Censoring is a special form of Fixation, bordering on mental masochism: we field or create a great idea, we recognize it as such, but deny or kill it anyway. I often think of it as "ideacide."

Whether it's because we're too critical or because we recoil at the impending pain of change and disruption of normalcy, Self-Censoring arises out of fear. That fear shrinks us, mentally. We lose our childlike, uncensored urge to play, explore, and experiment. We render ourselves mindless. When that happens, we are vulnerable to our other thinking flaws, such as Fixation and Overthinking, which become both judge and jury. Then we slap ourselves on the forehead when someone else "steals" our great idea.

I know for a fact that the elegant solution to the thought challenge exists among the participants and is often suggested in small team discussions far more times than it is selected as the best idea. I distinctly saw one of the bomb techs slap his teammate on the arm and whisper through gritted teeth: "I knew we should just take the tops off!"

Being what I consider the deadliest of the fatal flaws, Self-Censoring requires a potent fix, one which has foundations in the larger and broader concept of mindful awareness, or mindfulness for short. Not to be confused with Asian meditation-based philosophies seeking to suspend thinking, mindfulness is active thinking centered on achieving a higher order of attention, considering different perspectives, and noticing moment-to-moment changes around you. David Rock, in his book *Your Brain At Work*, defines it as "living in the present, being aware of experience as it occurs in real time, and accepting what you see."

The fix for Self-Censoring is based on a classic tool, introduced by philosopher Adam Smith over a century and a half ago, which he called "The Impartial Spectator." It is a method for attuning your attention in a way that indeed puts you in the present and gives you a more unbiased perspective, in much the way our attention is focused when we travel to a new place. As visitors we are outsiders looking in: naturally mindful, fully present, noticing details the locals now take for granted. Psychologists refer to it as *self-distancing*, and as the name implies, the concept is one of distancing yourself from, well, you. Researchers at the University of Michigan recently discovered that the simple practice of replacing the first-person pronoun "I" with either the third-person pronoun "You" or their own name in working through a stressful situation reduced anxiety, rumination, and what athletes call "choking."[3]

Thus the seventh fix: *Self-Distancing*.

## WINNING THE BRAIN GAME

### Fixing the Seven Fatal Flaws of Thinking

| FLAW | FIX |
|---|---|
| Leaping | Framestorming |
| Fixation | Inversion |
| Overthinking | Prototesting |
| Satisficing | Synthesis |
| Downgrading | Jumpstarting |
| NIH *(Not Invented Here)* | PFE *(Proudly Found Elsewhere)* |
| Self-Censoring | Self-Distancing |

Leaping, Fixation, and Overthinking make up Part One of this book, which I'm calling *Misleading*, because of the power these flaws have to lead us astray. Part Two looks at Satisficing and Downgrading, and is labeled *Mediocre*, because these two flaws undercut our best thinking and performance. Part Three covers NIH and Self-Censoring, which from my observation and experience are not quite as dominant and prevalent as the others, but certainly equally as deadly, if not deadlier, and are properly classified as *Mindless*.

In reality, all seven of these thinking flaws are not truly separate and distinct, but rather interrelated variations on a general tendency to let our lazy brains take over and orchestrate the symphony of thought our minds are capable of. Regardless of playing field, I believe mindful thinking is the new competitive advantage, and the seven fixes are a magic set of tools for achieving it. In my work with professionals and organizations of all kinds, I have found them to be best in class. The seven can all be placed in a larger toolbox properly labeled *Reframing*.

Reframing is the singular response to the question of how to respond to our mantra, which as you may recall is: *what appears to be the problem, isn't; what appears to be the solution, isn't; what appears to be impossible, isn't.*

So what happened in your own problem-solving? If you didn't arrive at the actual and elegant solution as your best idea, my bet is that you got tripped up by one of the seven fatal thinking flaws, just like the LAPD bomb squad. If you did in fact arrive at the elegant solution, you are to be congratulated. Give this book to a friend. You don't need it, and I can't help you.

Back to my story.

As I explained these mental "glitches" to the bomb techs, they began to loosen up and lean in. They chimed in with examples of how these various traps had played out on the job and even in their personal lives. They arrived at the desired conclusion: don't let these traps prevent the new strategy from being anything less than elegant.

In the end, the 12 bomb techs created an altogether new, far more fluid way to respond to bomb threats. They presented the concept to their commanders, and after some field tests and a few months of tweaking, it became the new standard for the Los Angeles Police Department.* Would they have done so without a little off-road thinking activity? Perhaps. But previous attempts hadn't made much headway, and I like to think I helped the team in some small way.

Fast forward to the following year. I'm on the sixth floor of LAPD's Parker Center,† with then-Chief William Bratton and his rather large staff of nearly 20 assistant chiefs, deputy chiefs, and special commanders, including current LAPD Chief Charlie Beck, along with the department psychologist. They liked what had happened with the bomb squad. They want to think through a new strategy using the same approach. I start them off with another thinking challenge.‡ They experience the same kinds of results as the bomb squad. They too learn how to fix the seven fatal thinking flaws, eventually creating a new and elegant top tier operational strategy for enforcing the law in Los Angeles.

Fast-forward to the present day, over 10 years and several hundreds of thought challenges given to many thousands of people after that day in 2005, in which I now have enough evidence, arsenal, and guidance from several world-class thinkers I'm fortunate to count as close advisors that I can now offer you this little crash course in winning the brain game.

---

* For reasons of security and confidentiality, I am unable to share the beautifully elegant and simple visual created by the LAPD Bomb Squad.

† The old Parker Center, not the new one opened in 2009.

‡ I will share this exercise with you in the next chapter.

PART ONE

# Misleading

## CHAPTER 1

# Leaping

> *If I had an hour to solve a problem and my life*
> *depended on the solution, I would spend the first fifty-*
> *five minutes determining the proper question to ask,*
> *for once I know the proper question, I could solve the*
> *problem in less than five minutes.*
>
> **—ALBERT EINSTEIN**

When we're toddlers, we have all the time in the world. Days last forever. Everything fascinates us. The world is filled with wonder. Our urge to explore and play fuels our curiosity, which is all-consuming. We are sponges, hungry to experience everything around us, immersing ourselves in our environment in every way possible, with all of our senses. Put us in the sandbox with a cup and spoon and we will occupy ourselves for hours, content to play until we get tired, thirsty, or hungry. Our brains soak it all in, wiring thousands of new connections each day, creating new knowledge. As we gain language skills, our curiosity takes the form of incessant questions, unbound and uncensored. Then, in preschool, our activity becomes more structured. We learn about rules: sitting up straight, coloring inside the lines, resting on cue, speaking in turn, standing in lines, and, of course, never talking when we're in one. In elementary school, we learn the importance of answering the teacher's questions correctly within strict time limits. Our performance depends on it: we're graded on our ability to regurgitate quickly. As we move up in grade, all of that gets exaggerated, enforced, and accelerated, year after year. Our own questions lose priority, until we eventually lose our desire to ask at all, for fear of disrupting others. As we enter the workforce, we bring with us this embedded *right-answer-now!* mindset, which pleases the boss, who has taken the place our teachers once held. By the time we're 25, we're finely tuned, well-oiled machines of efficiency, wired to answer quickly and, if we're lucky, correctly.

Given our grooming, is it any wonder that we leap to solutions?

## THE LEAPING FLAW

Psychologists give Leaping any number of labels, from the more sophisticated "rapid cognition" to the more colloquial JTC, which stands for "jumping to conclusions." Malcolm Gladwell called it "thin-slicing" in his 2005 book *Blink: The Power of Thinking Without Thinking*, the genesis for which actually concerned an incident he had with some New York Police Department officers, whom he thanks in his acknowledgments.

As he tells it, he had grown his hair long after his megahit *The Tipping Point*, which for most people is inconsequential. Not for Malcolm . . . his hair is even more wild in person than it looks in pictures.* All of a sudden, he was getting

---

* I met and spoke with Malcolm Gladwell several years ago when we were both speaking at the CA World Conference in Las Vegas. I was the warmup band.

all the wrong kinds of attention from authorities—traffic stops, airport security pat-downs—which culminated in his being stopped for questioning by three NYPD officers as he strolled down 14th Street in Manhattan. They were looking for a felony perpetrator, the defining quality of whom was a "big head of curly hair." The officers had driven their van up on the sidewalk and jumped out on nothing more than a glance at Malcolm's head. It took a full 20 minutes before the officers set him free, even though he had nothing whatsoever in common with the police artist's sketch, other than hairstyle. "Something about that first impression created by my hair derailed every other consideration in the hunt for the rapist," Gladwell wrote. "That episode on the street got me thinking about the weird power of first impressions. And that thinking led to *Blink*—so I suppose, before I thank anyone else, I should thank those three police officers."[4]

*Blink* was published right in the midst of my work with the LAPD bomb squad, so the timing couldn't have been more perfect. I shared the story with the officers I worked with in follow-up sessions, and we all agreed that no matter how trained and skilled someone might be, everyone falls prey to Leaping. They actually had their own term for it: *jumping the gun*. In fact, they decided to give me a taste of my own medicine, which actually involved a gun. They invited me to Elysian Park, home to the LAPD Academy. And oh did they ever exact revenge for the shampoo exercise.

The gun I was given didn't fire real bullets, thankfully. It was wired to some sort of video training device. In front of me was a large screen. After some cursory instruction on how to hold, aim, and fire the weapon, the fun began. A video began to play, from my point of view. In other words, it was as if I was a police officer wearing a GoPro. In the first situation, I've stopped a suspect car, the driver of which is wanted for questioning. As I approach the car, the driver gets out, reaches into his jacket pocket, and before I can even react, he's stabbed me in the gut. I'm down. They play it again, and this time I'm ready. As the driver reaches into his jacket pocket, I shoot him in the shoulder. Turns out he was just getting his wallet.

Over and over, through a succession of look-alike situations in which I really do need to "blink" rather than "think" my way through simply to survive, I come to understand the incredibly difficult and complex tension between the two modes. I come to appreciate the enormous pressure one can feel when placed in potentially life-threatening situations that can transpire in a millisecond. And I come to understand that blinking and thinking are two sides of the same coin. The challenge is in training our minds to be more effective in applying either or both, as the situation dictates.

As I left my bomb squad officers rolling on the floor laughing at my dismal display of paramilitary potential, a question began taking shape in my mind: *How might we exploit our inclination to blink to improve our ability to think?*

## WHY WE LEAP

That question drove me to investigate the connections between mind and brain, as well as mind and body. It also enabled me to find and eventually use a different kind of thought challenge, a more physical one, and one that I used with Chief Bratton and his deputies and commanders.

Now, there is perhaps nothing more satisfying than putting a police officer in handcuffs and watching them try to escape. Which is exactly what I did. I found something eerily appropriate called "The Prisoner's Release," from an 1896 book called *Cassell's Complete Book of Sports and Pastimes*:

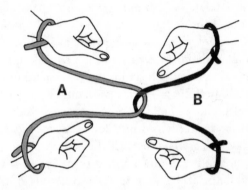

Take two pieces of string, and round the wrists of two persons tie
the string, as shown. The puzzle is for them to liberate themselves,
or for any one else to release them without untying the string.*

I went to Home Depot, got some different colored nylon rope, and made five pairs of handcuffs, and with uncontainable joy presented the challenge to LAPD's highest ranking echelon. I gave them five minutes to escape, impressing upon them the constraints: the handcuffs must remain on the original wrists at all times . . . no removal allowed.

---

* The original directions also include: "It adds to the amusement of the puzzle if one of the persons is a lady and the other a gentleman." I've tried this. They are correct.

In a magnificent display of Leaping, each couple immediately and without a moment's hesitation leapt into various versions of the same solution. I call it string dancing: stepping over the ropes, sliding them up and over themselves as they twirl and twist and struggle to get free. Over the course of the five minutes, not only did no one escape, but all of the other fatal flaws of thinking gloriously manifested themselves: they kept doing different versions of the same move (Fixation), they went through gyrations, twists, and turns that tangled them up even more (Overthinking). Halfway through, as exasperation set in, I gave them a hint: "You do not need to perform any dance movements . . . you can solve the problem face to face without a single twist or turn." They stopped momentarily to listen, looked at me like I had two heads, looked at their partner, looked at their handcuffs, shrugged, and then immediately returned to what they were doing before (NIH). Soon they began asking if they could cut the ropes or swap hands since it wasn't explicitly stated that they couldn't (Satisficing), asking me if this is even possible (Downgrading), and even overriding their partner who might say something like, "let's try a different way" or "let's think this through" (Self-Censoring).

To this day, I use this as the icebreaker to a one-day bootcamp I deliver twice a year at the California Peace Officer Standards and Training Command College, in a program for senior police executives aspiring to become a chief of police in a California city. The results are similar, with roughly one out of every 20 or so couples escaping the handcuffs elegantly. Each time that happens, it becomes clearer to me that the key to success is to hold off on "the dance," and think about the problem first before taking any action whatsoever.

Doing so enables the escape in just a few seconds, while the dancers continue to dance, with ever increasing levels of frustration.*

Perhaps the easiest way to explain Leaping is to do what psychologists and neuroscientists alike do: categorize our thinking into two main circuits. Psychologist Daniel Kahneman in his 2011 book *Thinking, Fast and Slow* uses terms coined by psychologists Keith Stanovich and Richard West: System 1 and System 2. There are many other labels for these circuits, such as automatic and controlled, left and right brain, default and executive drive, conscious and unconscious thinking, working and latent memory, divergent and convergent thinking, basal ganglia and prefrontal cortex, etc. Let's just keep it simple and memorable, taking our cues from Kahneman: FAST and SLOW. Let's be clear that our brain is far more complex than this, and this two-circuit concept is simply a helpful metaphor that aids a short discussion.

---

* The solution in Cassell's is: "B makes a loop of his string, passes it under either of A's manacles, slips it over A's hand, and both will be free. Reverse the proceeding, and the manacles are again as before."

FAST does the rapid, automatic, reactive, unconscious, and instinctive thinking we employ to solve routine problems . . . Gladwell's "blink." SLOW handles the labored, effortful, conscious, and rational thinking we employ to solve more complex and unfamiliar challenges.

Here's how it all works. When I toss a ball to you, you don't need to think deeply about it in order to catch it. FAST, operating on "heuristics," or patterns, guides your automatic response of quickly positioning your hands exactly where they need to be and clutching the ball as it lands right where you know it will. But if it happens to be the very first time anyone has ever tossed you a ball, it's SLOW that will handle things, and you'll drop the ball. You indeed have to think about it at first, deliberately and consciously trying to catch it until you "get it" and your brain forms a pattern, enabling FAST to work.

FAST is where our expertise and confidence live, where our intuitive "sixth sense" operates. It's also where almost all of our mistakes get made. And it's where Leaping occurs. Kahneman tells us that our FAST circuit is a "machine for jumping to conclusions" when information is limited. This is exactly what Malcolm Gladwell experienced with the three NYPD officers.

For example, suppose I ask you whether you think Nancy would be a great nurse. I tell you that she is caring, empathetic, and meticulous. You've probably already leapt to a yes, thanks to FAST, which reads that bit of information as all good signs, which of course they are. Still, you leapt. You did not bother to stop and ask what the critical qualities of a good nurse might be. What if I was just about to tell you that Nancy is a kleptomaniac, hot-tempered, and suffers occasional memory loss? None of this new information conflicts with the first three traits I gave you, but you probably don't want Nancy as your nurse any longer.

## THE NEUROSCIENCE OF LEAPING

In a recent study[5] published in the April 2015 edition of *PLoS Biology*, researchers at the California Institute of Technology (Caltech) discovered the source of why we jump to conclusions: uncertainty. When we are unsure of a situation, we quickly, and often erroneously, associate cause and effect. The authors use the term "one-shot learning" to describe jumping to conclusions.

"If you are uncertain, or lack evidence, about whether a particular outcome was caused by a preceding event, you are more likely to quickly associate them together," says Sang Wan Lee, a postdoctoral scholar in neuroscience at Caltech and lead author of the study. "Many have assumed that the novelty of a stimulus would be the main factor driving one-shot learning, but our computational model showed that causal uncertainty was more important."

Using a simple behavioral task paired with brain imaging, the researchers were able to determine where in the brain this causal processing takes place and pinpoint the part responsible for triggering one-shot learning. A part of the prefrontal cortex—the large brain area located immediately behind the forehead that is associated with complex cognitive activities—appears to evaluate such causal uncertainty and then couple with the hippocampus to switch on one-shot learning when needed.

*(continued)*

"A switch is an appropriate metaphor," says coauthor Shinsuke Shimojo. Since the hippocampus is known to be involved in so-called episodic memory, in which the brain quickly links a particular context with an event, the researchers hypothesized that this brain region might play a role in jumping to conclusions. But they were surprised to find that the coupling between the prefrontal cortex and the hippocampus was either all or nothing. "Like a light switch, one-shot learning is either on, or it's off."

The researchers were intrigued by the fact that this part of the prefrontal cortex is very close to another part of the prefrontal cortex that they previously found to be involved in helping the brain to switch between two other forms of learning—habitual and goal-directed learning, which involve routine behavior and more carefully considered actions, respectively.

The researchers cautiously speculated that a significant function of the prefrontal cortex is to act as a leader, telling other parts of the brain involved in different types of behavioral functions when they should get involved and when they shouldn't.

FAST is what allows us to not only make it through the day with ease and efficiency, but performs effortlessly and highly effectively most of the time, especially when it comes to familiar situations and routine problems. No one wants or needs to think deeply about walking, shaving, or driving to work . . . we'd never get anything done!

But FAST makes mistakes. That's where SLOW comes in. The problem is that while deeper thinking SLOW should be the one that prevents those mistakes and keeps us out of trouble, it's lazy. It wants to act like FAST. SLOW thinking is just plain hard work, requiring too much mental and physical effort. And our formative years have not focused on thinking slow, but rather how to economize thinking to make it fast. All the math, language, and science skills we learn in school are really just handy proxies for thinking. If you're taking action of any kind, FAST rules. SLOW kicks in only when FAST has run out of possible alternatives. The tension between the two systems is quite dramatic, and plays out every day of our lives.

Take the case of the TV remote control. You plop down on the couch after a long day, eager to watch television. FAST kicks in, and you automatically grab the remote, aim it at the box, and hit the power button. But the TV doesn't come on. What do you do? If you're like me, you keep hitting the power button. You try different angles, maybe wiping the infrared sensor on your sleeve, all the while hitting the power button. That's your FAST beginning its run through known fixes. It knows what to do next: play with the batteries. You don't replace them, you roll them around, because just the thought of getting up off the couch and having to rummage around in the kitchen utility drawer in search of four AAA batteries that probably aren't there—because that would have required some SLOW thinking ahead— is unpleasant. But the battery roll fails, and you have to change them, which you do. Then you start all over, aiming and pressing the power button. But the TV still doesn't turn on. SLOW finally kicks in, but only because you've exhausted every known fix, and you're forced into deeper thinking, which almost always begins with a question. In this case, why isn't this thing working?

Unfortunately, SLOW is the system of last resort. When it comes to the more complex problems, FAST leads us astray, gets in the way, and prevents us from solving them. By nature, the mind stays closed as long as possible!

## LEAP AND LOSE

Suppose you're playing a video game that gives you a choice: fight the alien superwarrior or three human soldiers in a row. The game informs you that your chances of defeating the alien superwarrior are 1 in 7. But your chances of defeating a human soldier are 50-50. What do you do? Most people would automatically fight the human soldiers. It seems to make intuitive sense, the odds seem to be in your favor.

But they're not. Your probability of beating the three soldiers in a row would be $\frac{1}{2} \times \frac{1}{2} \times \frac{1}{2}$, or $\frac{1}{8}$. In other words, you had a better shot ($\frac{1}{7}$) at beating the alien superwarrior.

You leap, you lose.

So what can we do to improve the tension between FAST and SLOW?

Daniel Kahneman isn't much help, advising us that "The best we can do is a compromise: learn to recognize situations in which mistakes are likely and try harder to avoid significant mistakes when the stakes are high."

I believe we can do far better than simply compromise. I am confident we can leverage our FAST circuit to improve our SLOW, and train our minds to fix our brain's fatal flaw of Leaping. The clues are in the Caltech study cited earlier, which supports what I have observed and experienced in the last 10 years working with hundreds of problem-solving teams.

The secret lies in how to trigger SLOW so that it acts and feels like FAST.

## THE FIX: FRAMESTORMING

If I have learned anything from facilitating problem-solving sessions, it is that we will be largely unsuccessful in attempting to shut off the Leaping impulse, and we should not even try. We will make far more progress if we instead redirect and channel the instinct to act into behavior that feels like brainstorming,* but involves generating questions instead of answers.

It's called *framestorming*, a mash-up of framing and brainstorming. It's a way to change behavior without the pain of change, and it works amazingly well. Framestorming is more like *aikido* in martial arts, which uses opposing forces to one's advantage, rechanneling and redirecting them; it's less like *karate*, which uses one's brute force in the form of punches and kicks to win a confrontation. Aikido means "way of balanced life energy," which really gets to the heart of what framestorming achieves: a better balance between FAST and SLOW thinking energy.

Framestorming operates under the same basic rules of brainstorming, which are well-known and well over a half

---

* The rules of brainstorming are widely documented, so they do not need to be detailed here.

century old: go for quantity, build on ideas, withhold judgment. That's the *storming* part. It's the part that feels good,
because it calls up FAST. What about the *frame* part?

Musician Frank Zappa perhaps put it best when he said:
"The most important thing in art is the frame. For paint,
literally. For other arts, figuratively—because, without this
humble appliance, you can't know where the art stops and
the real world begins."

What Zappa meant is that how we frame something has
everything to do with how well it turns out, and that framing
is as much an art as art itself. We frame art to draw attention
to the picture. A great frame enhances appreciation. A picture isn't complete without it. But most of us probably don't
pay much attention to the frame. Unless, of course, it isn't
there. In which case we probably find it a bit tougher to give
the piece its proper consideration.

Framing in problem-solving is every bit as important, and works much the same way. The ability to properly
frame an issue or problem goes far in avoiding the typical
pitfalls that limit our ability to reach the elegant solution.
But we're not as good at it as we could be, for several reasons relating to the tension between FAST and SLOW. We're
impatient, with attention spans sometimes far too limited
to put the required energy toward framing. We're obsessed
with solutions, but not with the process of generating the
optimal one. We're fond of common sense, which doesn't
always square with proper framing. And we have a flair for
the obvious, mostly because it provides a suitable mental
shortcut. We're deluged with routine problems every day
that don't require framing, merely quick workarounds via
FAST thinking, so our natural tendency is to treat complex

problems requiring SLOW thinking with our preferred FAST thinking.

In my observations of all the people I've seen work on the kinds of thought exercises I've shared with you, framing rarely occurs. Almost everyone moves right into tossing up ideas in the mistaken belief that I've given them all of the information they need. They bypass the critical step involving the frame. They certainly don't consider multiple frames. The reason they don't stop is clear: it's the stopping itself that feels uncomfortable. Remember, calling up SLOW is the last thing we want to do!

The best tool for fixing the Leaping flaw is framestorming. You do it right before brainstorming . . . always, every time. It will come easily and comfortably, because it feels like Leaping. Except with framestorming, the focus is on generating questions, not solutions.

The power of framestorming lies in its ability to engage our SLOW thinking in a manner that feels like FAST thinking. At the same time, it turns problems into puzzles. When we view something as a problem, we naturally engage in Leaping to solutions. When something is a puzzle, though, we naturally slow down a bit: we learn at an early age when doing puzzles that we need to get the corners and edges down first. Getting the puzzle frame right is half the battle!

## Framestorming in Three Easy Steps

Framestorming consists of three straightforward steps conducted under the general rules of brainstorming, with the ultimate goal of stating the challenge as a compelling question that acts to frame a problem as an intriguing puzzle, one that engages our more imaginative SLOW thinking.

***Step 1: Cue the language of frames.***

Good frames are stated as questions. Friend and fellow author Warren Berger wrote what I consider to be the definitive treatment of the language of frames in his book *A More Beautiful Question*. In it he argues that while we're all hungry for better answers, we must first learn to ask the right questions, then proceeds to demonstrate through a number of well-researched stories that the most creative, successful people in the world tend to be expert questioners. They've mastered the art of inquiry, raising questions no one else is asking—and finding the answers everyone else is seeking.

As Warren defines it, "a beautiful question is an ambitious yet actionable question that can begin to shift the way we perceive or think about something—and that might serve as a catalyst to bring about change."[6]

## A BEAUTIFUL QUESTION

An ambitious yet actionable question that can begin to shift the way we perceive or think about something—and that might serve as a catalyst to bring about change.

In my interview with Berger,[7] I asked him who in business does the best job of asking beautiful questions. His answer: "Entrepreneurs, or at least the successful ones. They almost have no choice . . . their whole reason for being is to disrupt, innovate, and solve a problem no one else is solving. But first they have to define and frame the problem, and that's usually done through smart questioning."

For example, Netflix founder Reed Hastings asked, *why should I have to pay late fees for renting videos?* Square founder Jack Dorsey asked, *why can't individuals accept credit cards?* And it was Polaroid founder Edwin Land's three-year-old daughter Jennifer who famously asked, *why do we have to wait for the picture?*

Warren advises cycling through three stages of inquiry:

1. Why?
2. What if?
3. How?

"As I studied innovation stories," he told me, "I found that questioners often started by trying to understand and frame a problem—and that tends to involve a lot of why questions. Why is this a problem? Why hasn't anyone solved it? Why might it represent an opportunity? At some point, the innovator moves from why to what if questions—imagining possible solutions, often by connecting ideas. What if we tried X? What if we combined Y with Z? That's the idea stage. Then, you have to get from imaginative, what if possibilities to something more practical and concrete; you begin to ask, how might we do this?"

Rarely in watching thousands of people grappling with a thought exercise do I observe questions of any kind get raised, much less beautiful ones.

### Step 2: Generate questions.
Now generate as many *Why? What if?* and *How?* questions as you can. As in brainstorming, framestorming initially favors quantity over quality. Go for at least a dozen questions that

frame the challenge, preferably more. Don't stop until you're well into the double digits.

Take the advice of Albert Einstein: "Life is like riding a bicycle. To keep your balance you must keep moving." This is what your FAST thinking lives for, so go with the flow. Reserve judgment or evaluation for step three—the last thing you want to do at this point is be conservative or critical.

In thinking about the shampoo theft problem from the Introduction, a quick framestorming activity might have yielded a dozen or so questions such as: *Why are people stealing the shampoo? Why doesn't everyone steal the shampoo? Why haven't previous solutions worked? Why is the shampoo so appealing? Why is it so easy to steal the shampoo? Why are people so tempted to steal the shampoo bottle? What if we did nothing? What if no one wanted to steal the shampoo? What if you couldn't hide the shampoo in your gym bag? What if the shampoo didn't travel well? What if the bottle was hard to move? How might we make it impossible to steal shampoo? How might we make people hate to steal the shampoo? How might we make it dangerous to steal shampoo? How might we remove temptation? How might we redesign the shampoo bottle without cost?*

Note that none of these are solutions, but rather provocative precursors, some of which may immediately spark a solution that meets the constraints of the challenge. All of them challenge the original question of how to stop people from stealing without it costing a penny. As my friend and Stanford creativity professor Tina Seelig says, "Start by questioning the question you're asking in the first place. Your answer is baked into your question."

### Step 3: Pick the two best.

Once you have a master list of frames, you can select at least two that will launch you into the solution brainstorming mode, which is essentially another round of the *Why? What if?* and *How?* questions, this time focused on answers. From there, you know what to do!

You should be aware that framestorming, while being a powerful antidote to Leaping, does not guarantee the elegant solution, but it will increase the odds of putting your best brain forward.

---

**TAKEAWAY** | ## The Flaw & The Fix

### LEAPING

Leaping to solutions when tackling a complex challenge is natural and intuitive, but almost never results in an elegant solution. By inserting a simple step called framestorming that feels equally intuitive but is focused on questions rather than answers, we can trigger our deeper and more creative thinking circuits.

## CHAPTER 2

# Fixation

*Reality is merely an illusion, albeit a very*
*persistent one.*

**—ALBERT EINSTEIN**

An unemployed woman who did not have her driver's license with her failed to stop at a railroad crossing, then ignored a one-way traffic sign and traveled three blocks in the wrong direction down the one-way street. All this was observed by a nearby police officer, who was on duty, yet made no effort to issue the woman a ticket for violating the laws. Why?

A man leaves for a horsepacking trip on Sunday. He returns on Sunday, yet was gone for exactly 10 straight days, without crossing international date lines. How is this possible?

A young boy turned off the lights in his bedroom and managed to get into bed before the room was dark. If the bed is ten feet from the light switch and the light bulb and he used no wires, strings, or other contraptions to turn off the light, how did he do it?

Mr. Hardy was washing windows on a high-rise office building when he slipped and fell off a 60-foot ladder onto the concrete sidewalk below. Incredibly, he did not injure himself in any way. How is this possible?

Can you identify the pattern in the following letters?

A E F H I K L M N T V W X Y Z B C D G J O P Q R S U

Can you think of a word that forms a phrase with each of the following words: *shot*, *plate*, and *broken*?

Move a single stick to correct the incorrect Roman numeral equation: ||| + ||| = |||

There are three switches outside a closed room. There are three lamps inside the room. You can flip the switches as much as you want while the door is closed, but then you must enter just once and determine which switch is connected to which lamp. How can you do it?

A dealer in antique coins got an offer to buy a beautiful bronze coin. The coin had an emperor's head on one side and the date 544 BC stamped on the other. The dealer examined the coin, but instead of buying it, he called the police. Why?

Juliette and Jennifer were born on the same day of the same month of the same year to the same mother and the same father, yet they are not twins. How is that possible?

Can you rearrange the letters n-e-w-d-o-o-r to make one word?

A prisoner was attempting to escape from a tower. He found in his cell a rope which was only half the length needed to reach the ground safely. He divided the rope in half, tied the two parts together, and escaped. How could he have done this?

A giant inverted steel pyramid is perfectly balanced on its point. Any movement of the pyramid will cause it to topple over. Underneath the point of the pyramid is a $100 bill. How could you remove the bill without disturbing the pyramid?

In what direction is the bus pictured below facing, left or right?

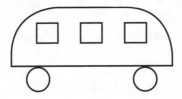

Show how you can make the triangle below point downward by moving only three of the circles.

These 15 brainteasers are the kind of problems psychologists and neuroscientists love to give their research subjects in the lab, often hooked up to fMRI scanners, in order to test whether they have an *Aha!* moment, and if they do, how long it takes, and if they don't, what kinds of hints induce it. Researchers have been using these types of insight problems for nearly 100 years. If you weren't successful in solving them, don't be discouraged; the average success rate among those who have never seen these classic problems before hovers around 50 percent, with many failing completely, depending on the problem.[8]

I've put the solutions in the back of the book, if you wish to indulge in the Downgrading flaw (see Introduction) and preemptively surrender. In the meantime, know that if these problems stumped you for the most part like they did me, it's just our Fixation flaw working in high gear.

## THE FIXATION FLAW

Psychologist Karl Duncker in his 1939 book *On Problem Solving* coined the term "functional fixedness" to explain the difficulty people have in looking at objects and situations in ways different than they commonly do, or have in the past. Ever since, researchers have been using updated versions of the kinds of problems he used to study different ways to trigger the kind of thinking that defeats functional fixedness, often referred to as "sudden creative insight," what we call the *Eureka!* or *Aha!* moment.* Various other labels for functional fixedness include paradigms, blind spots, mindset, bias, brain lock, and mental models. Let's again keep it simple: Fixation.

---

* The most famous and most cited in articles and books is known as the Duncker candle problem. Subjects are given a candle, a box of thumbtacks, and a box of matches, and asked to "fix the lit candle to the wall so that it will not drip wax onto the table below." Participants either get it right away, or struggle for over 10 minutes, often failing to solve the problem, the solution to which is to empty the box of thumbtacks, put the candle in the box, use the thumbtacks to nail the box with the candle in it to the wall, and light the candle with a match. "Functional fixedness" prevents participants from seeing the box as anything other than a device to hold the thumbtacks.

Outside the safety of psychological experiments, Fixation can wreak havoc in individuals, organizations, and even entire industries.

Dr. Jeffrey Schwartz, MD,* who will help us to understand the neuroscience of the thinking flaws throughout this book, is a neuropsychiatrist who has devoted his life to an extreme form of Fixation: obsessive-compulsive disorder (OCD). By all accounts, OCD is a devastating, self-destructive disease involving biochemical imbalance in the brain, but Schwartz uses a process he developed at UCLA which uses self-directed neuroplasticity to help patients use the power of their minds to break the stranglehold their brains have on how they function day to day.†

Organizational theorist Ian Mitroff attributes General Motors' dramatic loss of market share in the 1980s at the hands of import car companies to a decades-old, multilevel version of Fixation that went something like this: *styling and status is more important than quality, foreign cars are no threat, and workers don't make a difference.* General Motors only became aware of their faulty thinking when it was far too late.

For nearly a century during the 1800s, the ice industry revolved around a simple function: *harvesting*. Dozens of strong men used large saws designed to cut large blocks of ice from frozen lakes and rivers and hauled the blocks by horse

---

* Jeffrey Schwartz has coauthored several bestselling books, including *The Mind and the Brain, Brainlock*, and, most recently, *You Are Not Your Brain*. I first met him in 2008 when I was researching *In Pursuit of Elegance*.

† I will say more about this process when I discuss the fix for Fixation. Neuroplasticity refers to the ability to use mental activity to change physical brain circuitry.

and wagon to ice houses for storage or to barges and trains for shipping. The ice industry spurred the rapid growth in a range of other U.S. industries, including meat, produce, and fish that previously were restricted to local consumption. Ice harvesting created an American "cooling culture," and most households had an icebox for storing perishables. The ice harvesting trade continued to grow and spread to become a global market by the end of the 1800s, peaking in 1900. *Then it vanished nearly overnight.* Harvesting was replaced by a new function, ice manufacturing, which had slowly been developing in the late 1800s. Ice plants with mechanically powered chilling facilities that could produce ice blocks quickly and cheaply all year round put the ice harvesters out of business. Ice factories sprung up in every city, and ice manufacturing enjoyed a profitable existence for nearly a quarter century. *Then it nearly vanished overnight.* A new function, refrigeration, replaced ice manufacturing. Refrigeration absorbed ice making and made cold storage—in the form of electric powered freezers and refrigerators—a household convenience.

Here's the thing: none of the ice harvesters became ice manufacturers. And none of the ice manufacturers became refrigeration companies. The reason? They were fixed in their function, locked into the activity they performed, unable to see the bigger picture and the changes happening around them, or choosing to ignore them even if they did.

They were victims of Fixation.

It would be ever so much easier for us all if we could simply switch on the Apple tagline "think different" on demand. But we can't, and no such switch exists. Each of us has a robust set of unconscious thinking patterns that figure centrally into how we look at any challenge. Fixation is one of the most prevalent: it has never once failed to appear when I've given the kinds of thought exercises I've introduced you to in the previous two chapters. If Leaping is the foremost offender, Fixation is a close second. Framestorming (the fix for Leaping, as I hope you'll recall) is necessary but generally insufficient to address Fixation. Allow me to demonstrate by using another version of the thought challenge I used in the first chapter . . . again, not a sterile laboratory-type insight problem, but one based on a real case.

## ANOTHER REAL-WORLD THOUGHT CHALLENGE*

Imagine it's 1991, and you are the manager of the local video store, a branch of a larger chain. Back then, VCR machines didn't have the automatic rewind feature on them, and new media like DVDs and streaming video weren't even on the horizon. Your store has a problem: despite the fact that the rental contract clearly states that all videos must be rewound by the customer, 33 percent of your customers don't bother rewinding the tape. According to comment cards, this situation is a great source of customer dissatisfaction among the majority, your "conscientious

*(continued)*

---

* This problem is based on the true story of Star Video, which solved the issue many years ago. I had read a short discussion of the story in the 2003 book *Why Not?* (pp. 38, 116) by Barry Nalebuff and Ian Ayres, and turned it into a thought exercise. I first posed this problem in my 2009 book, *In Pursuit of Elegance: Why The Best Ideas Have Something Missing.*

rewinders." You've tried a number of things to solve the problem: incentives, penalties, "be kind, rewind" reminders—you've even installed a row of rewinding machines in the store. Nothing has improved the situation.

You decide to ask your employees, all of whom are hourly, to help solve the problem, and give them several non-negotiable conditions: The solution must achieve a level of 100 percent customer rewind accountability—it's the customer's responsibility, not the store's; there can be no additional burden on the customer; any solution must be of extremely low, and preferably no, cost—pennies per tape, at most; and the solution must be easy to implement, without disrupting the normal operation of the store. You tell your employees that they are free to be as innovative as they wish and do anything they want, as long as all conditions are met.

I hope you'll put the book down, refrain from Leaping, do a bit of Framestorming first, and try your hand at this version for five minutes. You'll at least double your chances of success in arriving at the elegant solution actually implemented, and I would not be surprised at all if you solved it well inside the five-minute mark if you Framestorm first. I'll even save you some frustration: don't bother inventing auto-rewind VCR, DVD, or streaming video—not only will you violate the conditions of the challenge, but they aren't necessary to solve it.

Now, the top 10 solutions participants give me, in no particular priority, are: a loyalty program that gives you a free rental if your rewind record is clean; a small monetary fine; more rewinders in the store with good signage; splicing reminders into the tape itself; altering either the video case or the cassette itself so that it won't fit back in the case if it hasn't been rewound; putting the movie on both sides of the tape; cutting the tape to put the ending at the front; eliminating the after-hours drop box; enlisting volunteers to rewind tapes in exchange for free rentals; and the all-time favorite: a drop box that rewinds the tape when it is inserted.

Unfortunately, each of these solutions violates one or more of the limitations I imposed, and furthermore, none of them solve the problem. If you look at them again, you may recognize a pattern: they are fixated on one primary function, which is returning a rewound tape to the store. But take a look at the problem again. It simply required the tape to be rewound; the issue of *when* the tape had to be rewound was never even mentioned, much less stipulated as a condition. That is Fixation in action. Your brain made an unconscious assumption that the tape had to be rewound before returning it, based on your experience in renting tapes; or if you're too young to remember the days of Blockbuster, based on stories of old folks like me who used to rent videotapes.

Perhaps in your framestorming effort you arrived at some helpful frames, such as "Why don't people rewind?" and "How do we make it impossible not to rewind?" The answer to the first is laziness. Once you understand that, you can see why previous solutions didn't work: nothing at such a low transaction level is going to change a basically lazy person into an accountable one. But you don't need to: the real issue revolves around making it impossible not to rewind the tape, and to do so with little or no cost and without placing additional burden on the customer.

The actual solution implemented by Star Video was to flip the policy and let the tapes be rented out un-rewound. They simply put a small sticker on the video case, stating that the tape may have to be rewound before watching. The solution placed no additional burden on the customer—one rewind was all that was ever required—and that didn't change. What changed is when the rewind occurred. If you got a tape that hadn't been rewound, you rewound it before watching. The stickers were very inexpensive, and there was no ongoing burden on the store. Problem solved. If you think about it, the solution is the same one most of us employ when doing laundry: we clean the lint screen *before* our next dryer load, not after the last one.

Let's take a look at how Fixation works.

## WHY WE FIXATE

Mst ppl cn ndrstntd ths sntnc wth lttl prblm. That's because the brain is a pattern-making, pattern-recognizing machine, and it immediately recognized and used the patterns in the letters to make sense of them, even though they didn't form words.

All day long, unbeknownst to us—and for the most part uncontrolled by us—our brains record every single experience, sending sensory information in the form of electrical impulses to our cerebral cortex, the "grey matter" that houses the brain's higher functions. Each new experience is automatically stored as data in our brain. The process is additive and cumulative, and generally goes unedited. Even though the electrical impulses themselves disappear in milliseconds, their passage to the nerve cells triggers a grouping mechanism, filing new information with other like data as it comes in, which in turn creates specific and unique patterns.

Different patterns combine to make memories and perceptions, and those connections are reinforced over time, becoming mental models—mindsets, biases, and paradigms. For the most part, these mental models allow us to function much more efficiently by helping us rapidly sift data and sort information into useful knowledge, according to whether it confirms or contradicts the strong patterns already embedded in our minds. There is no sophisticated term for this phenomenon; it's basically guesswork by the brain.

Fixation works in a couple of different ways. One way actually provokes the Leaping flaw. Former CIA analyst Morgan Jones uses the example below to demonstrate how it works. Can you guess who the individual might be in this description?

> A new chief executive, one of the youngest in
> his nation's history, is being sworn into office
> on a bleak, cold, cloudy day in January. He was
> raised as a Catholic. He rose to his new position
> in part because of his vibrant charisma. He is
> revered by the people and will play a crucial
> role in a military crisis that will face his nation.
> His name will become legendary.

The vast majority of people conclude that it is John F. Kennedy, and they arrive at their answer before the third sentence. That's your Fixation flaw hard at work, because there's another possibility: Adolph Hitler. When I give this description to a European audience, they answer Adolf

Hitler far more often. So what is going on here? In rather non-neuroscientific terms, as soon as our brain recognizes a piece of information as being part of a preexisting pattern, our FAST thinking overrides our SLOW, and we get fixed on our solution, essentially screening out other possibilities.

The other way Fixation works involves your brain making stuff up on its own. My favorite example\* enabling you to actually experience Fixation in action is to gaze at the three sets of right-angled lines below for a moment. I should tell you that they depict something so ubiquitous that you'd be hard-pressed to make it through the day without it. Can you identify it?

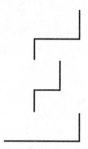

If you can't, it's because a key piece of information is missing. Once I share that hint with you, however, you will never again be able to see the image in quite the same way again.

Ready?

What you are looking at is the uppercase version of the most widely used letter in the English language. The letter,

---

\* I first introduced this exercise in my 2009 book *In Pursuit of Elegance* as a metaphorical example of an elegant solution.

though, exists in the white space. Do you see it now? It is the capital letter E. Look again. The black lines represent the shadow of the capital E. Please know that I did not create the E, your brain did, once it had just enough data to call up a well-worn pattern from memory.* And trust me, you will always see the E from now on.

But here is the Fixation power at work: try to unsee the E. Go back to the way you saw it a few seconds ago, when you were "innocent," without a bit of knowledge, and desperately trying to make sense of the lines, and looking at the image from a number of different perspectives.

Most people cannot unsee the E no matter how hard they try . . . even if they are successful for a split second, their brains flicker back to the E. What makes the image so indelible is the fact that your brain completed it. No "complete" E, no matter how elaborately or ornately rendered, could produce the same level of Fixation impact. Once you were given a clue, your brain created the image for you, without your having much say in the matter. The incomplete E took on a new form, a life of its own—one with real staying power.

## THE NEUROSCIENCE OF FIXATION

Neuroscience refers to three primary principles—Hebb's law, quantum Zeno effect, and attention density—to explain how enduring patterns are formed in the brain. Here's how Dr. Jeffrey Schwartz, MD, coauthor with Rebecca Gladding,

*(continued)*

---

* A very small percentage of people are never able to see the E in the white space. If that's you, do not worry, you do not suffer from brain damage.

MD, of *You Are Not Your Brain*, explained the first two to me.

## HEBB'S LAW

An easy way to remember Hebb's law is *"Neurons that fire together wire together,"* meaning that when groups of nerve cells are repeatedly activated at the same time, they form a circuit, and begin to work as one unit in lockstep fashion. Once the circuit is established, the brain regions involved in the circuit automatically respond in the same way every time a similar situation arises. This in turn causes the circuit to become stronger, and it is how habits are created and maintained.

## QUANTUM ZENO EFFECT

For Hebb's law to work, brain regions must not only activate, but *stay* activated at the same time. The activation happens as neurotransmitters that comprise the signals by which neurons communicate move through narrow channels only a single ion wide. That means our brain is a quantum space, and operates according to the laws of quantum mechanics. The quantum Zeno effect—described first in 1977 by physicist George Sudarshan—is what keeps the brain areas activated long enough.

Schwartz says that the quantum Zeno effect acts like a glue that holds brain circuits together in place in an activated state and stabilizes them long enough for Hebb's law to take effect. Once that happens, the brain is "hardwired," and responds to similar situations in repetitive patterns.

The mechanism for accomplishing this is called *attention density*, which we will discuss in Chapter 3.

The interesting question is, why are we so susceptible to our patterned thinking? Philosopher Immanuel Kant maintained that the mind is not built to give us raw knowledge of the world; we must always approach it from a special point of view, with a certain bias, to make it meaningful. The implication of this is that because mindsets represent our own unique view of the world, we instinctively rely on them to help us make sense of it. But these mindsets are hidden, hard to identify, and we defend them subconsciously.

Nearly a quarter century ago, the late Chris Argyris of Harvard University dove deep into our thinking patterns, eventually coining the term "mental models" as his preferred label of our own individual way of looking at the world. Argyris went so far as to say that many of our mental models are flawed, because most of what guides our behavior is related to one of four intentions: to remain in control, to maximize winning and minimize losing, to suppress negative feelings, and to be as rational as possible. He believed people act this way in order to avoid threat or embarrassment.

Argyris claimed that one's mental model plays out in a repetitive pattern he called the "ladder of inference." It works like this: You experience something, and that becomes the ladder's first rung. You apply your own theory to the situation, and that's the second rung. Next come the assumptions you make, the conclusions you draw, and the beliefs you hold. Finally, you act. But as you climb the ladder, you are becoming more and more abstract in your thought, further from the facts of the situation. And so you are vulnerable to less than optimal action, which helps explain why so many of our ideas and solutions don't meet the mark.

Because the process feeds back on itself, it strengthens the patterns in your mind, so the next time you're faced with a new situation, you're handicapped from the start.

## THE FIX: INVERSION

The cure for Fixation is what I call Inversion, because it involves flipping your thinking around in order see things through a new, fresh, and unique lens, in turn sparking new neural connections in your brain, effectively rewiring it. If this sounds even remotely like hocus-pocus mumbo-jumbo, rest assured that the ability of the mind to alter brain circuitry is about as scientifically proven as it can possibly get. It's called *neuroplasticity*, and it can be self-directed through various techniques.

For example, in helping OCD patients unlock their brains, Dr. Jeffrey Schwartz uses a four-step tool that involves reinterpreting and redirecting what he calls "deceptive brain messages" in order to overcome self-defeating thoughts and actions. The four steps—Relabel, Reframe, Refocus, Revalue—have proven to be a potent way for OCD patients to change their self-destructive perceptions. They first detach from the locked brain circuits that hold them prisoner, and then evoke and direct more beneficial thoughts toward healthy and helpful new patterns that achieve a complete shifting of mental gears that Schwartz likens to a manual but mindful override of the brain's automatic transmission. "The brain can exert a powerful grip on one's life—but only if you let it," states Schwartz. "The good news is you can overcome the brain's control and rewire your brain to work for you by learning to debunk the myths it has been so successfully selling you."

I figure if it can help unlock a brain as seized as that of an OCD patient, it most assuredly will help address our everyday Fixation. Schwartz's metaphor of shifting gears is indeed appropriate: Inversion is really thinking in reverse.

My favorite Inversion technique is one I learned several years ago while working with a few different industrial design firms, each of which had their own pet version of the method. No matter how it gets applied stylistically, the intent of the technique does not change, the essence of which is to shift us away from our current and probably fixed frame, turn things upside down and rightside round, and cut a few new and different thinking grooves.

## Inversion Method: "Opposite World"*

Opposite World is about inverting the normal conditions, defining features, or key characteristics of whatever challenge you're tackling. That inversion could involve, for example,

---

* Opposite World takes its cues from a 1992 episode of *Seinfeld* called "The Opposite," in which the character of George Costanza is in despair because every decision he's ever made in his entire life has been wrong: "My life is the complete opposite of everything I want it to be," he laments. Jerry Seinfeld suggests that if every instinct George has is wrong, the opposite would have to be right, whereupon George orders the opposite of his normal lunch, which catches the eye of a beautiful woman who has just ordered the same sandwich. George does the opposite of his natural instinct to lie, and tells her he's unemployed, broke, and lives at home. She becomes attracted to George and gets him an interview with her uncle who works for the Yankees. During the interview, George berates owner George Steinbrenner, which lands him his dream job and the ability to afford his own apartment. His entire life has turned around simply by doing the opposite of what his natural instinct would lead him to do.

*removal* of some sort (e.g., remove the top from a shampoo bottle, or remove the physical keyboard from a cell phone), *reversal* of an activity (e.g., videotapes leave the store unre-wound, or the chef decides what the diner will eat), or even a complete *exaggeration* or *escape* from reality that could border on pure fantasy (e.g., the camera only has one button, or people get paid for sleeping).

Once a list of opposites is developed, each item on the list becomes the starting point for a framestorm or brainstorm.

There are three basic steps.

### Step 1: List the defining attributes.

Let's take a common example, that of the traditional circus, first used by Stanford's Tina Seelig in teaching her entrepreneurship class how to address what she called "problem blindness" in her 2009 book, *What I Wish I Knew When I Was 20*.

The traditional circus has a number of classic elements:

> Clowns
> Barkers
> Multiple tents
> Carnival music
> "Star" attractions
> Animals
> Cheap tickets
> Kid oriented

***Step 2. For each element, list the extreme opposite or reverse.***
In our circus example:

| | |
|---|---|
| Clowns . . . . . . . . | **No clowns** |
| Barkers . . . . . . . . | **No barkers** |
| Multiple tents. . . . . | **One tent** |
| Carnival music . . . . | **Sophisticated music** |
| "Star" attractions . . . | **Ensemble cast** |
| Animals . . . . . . . . | **No animals** |
| Cheap tickets . . . . . | **Expensive tickets** |
| Kid oriented. . . . . . | **Adult oriented** |

Now, you probably just experienced a bit of the Fixation flaw, if by chance the thought of Cirque du Soleil popped into your head. That's your brain doing what it did with the JFK example earlier in the chapter. That's natural, of course. Part of the point here was indeed to illustrate the power of Inversion, an illustration which necessitates a backwards glance at something we consider nontraditional, even disruptive: Airbnb is the inverse of a traditional hotel or bed-and-breakfast in that it does not own property; Uber is the inverse of a traditional cab or limousine service, in that it does not have a fleet; Tesla cars are the inverse of cars with combustible engines, at least to some degree, in that they do not use gasoline for fuel.

The larger point, though, is that by taking the polar or extreme opposite view of the current or traditional way of thinking about a given concept, you can easily forge new avenues worth exploring creatively, which brings up the final step.

### Step 3: Framestorm/brainstorm, using the opposites as your starting point.

Look at your opposites list. While it may not reveal a solution, each opposite provides a starting point to now use your framestorming chops and ask *Why (not)? What if? How (might we)?* Those questions in turn will spark new trains of creative thought.

When you're done, you may be surprised at just how off-road you've gone with your thinking. A fun twist I've used is to think of the world's worst solution or strategy for the challenge you're tackling, then reversing each element of that idea. There are a number of different such twists and turns you can use, depending on the challenge and the people involved. The only constraint beyond those is your own imagination.

For example, I used a version of Opposite World with one group that wanted to change their organizational culture, aka "the ways things are done around here." I had them first list all the various "sacred cows"* of their organization: norms, procedures, rules, nonnegotiable elements of their current culture. They then thought of the extreme opposites of those elements, and a number of cultural shifts started immediately. For example, the sacred cow of "you must be in the office every day" was reversed to "you don't have to be in the office every day." That turned into a number of possibilities, the most important and lasting of which became the new normal: a results-only work environment, or ROWE.

---

* A "sacred cow" refers to a person or thing immune to criticism or questioning. The term alludes to the honored status of cows in Hinduism, where they are a symbol of God's generosity to humankind. It has been used figuratively for over 100 years, since about 1900.

In another case, I used a variation of this technique to conduct a visioning exercise with the senior executive team of a real estate development company during a management retreat just before the economic crisis of 2008. Things were going quite well at the time, and the real estate boom was in full swing, with nary a sign of impending doom. I'm certain it was nothing more than pure luck that instead of the typical exercise of envisioning what success would look like three years hence, I had them write a corporate obituary called "Rest In Peace," a kind of pre-mortem retrospective that detailed the key trials and tribulations, foibles and failures that led to the company's demise. I then had the team prioritize the list of issues and missteps according to its impact potential. Each of the priority items became the target of strategies to ensure that they did not actually happen in the future.

To this day, the CEO of the company* maintains that this exercise not only enabled the company to weather the downturn, but do so in way that positioned them to flourish once the economy emerged from its slumber.

---

* For purposes of confidentiality and competitive advantage, this company and its management team wishes to remain anonymous.

---

**TAKEAWAY** | # The Flaw & The Fix

## FIXATION

Our brains are masterful pattern machines, enabling us to function effectively and efficiently. Unfortunately, that patterned functioning can become so fixed that it becomes difficult to see things not as they are, but as they could be. By inverting the current reality, we can create new patterns and free up our thinking to explore possibility.

## CHAPTER 3

# Overthinking

*A person who never made a mistake never tried
anything new.*

—ALBERT EINSTEIN

n front of me sit 40 six sigma black belts,
appraising me warily, all squinty-eyed and
knit-browed. I've been asked to give them an
introduction to design thinking, which is an innovation
process enabling people who aren't trained in design to
employ a designer's sensibilities and tools to address a vast
range of challenges.* They're probably wary of me because I
don't have a six sigma belt of any color; in fact, I fully admit
to them that I wouldn't know the difference between a six
and any other number sigma. I flash back to when a team
of six sigma experts from a government organization came
through a Toyota facility and one of them, impressed with
what she saw, asked a manager how long he had been "doing
six sigma," to which he replied, "What is six sigma?"

My favorite introduction to design thinking is "The
Marshmallow Challenge," which was introduced by Peter
Skillman, a former designer with product design firm IDEO,

---

* Design thinking can be traced to the 1969 book *The Sciences of the Artificial*, by Herbert Simon, and has been popularized by design firm IDEO and
the Stanford Hassno Plattner Institute, aka the d school, where I received
my training in the method. The definition here is the one offered by IDEO.

at a TED conference in 2006. The exercise is this: a team of four people is given 18 minutes to construct the tallest free-standing structure from 20 sticks of straight spaghetti, a yard of masking tape, a yard of string, and a single marshmallow, which must be on top. You can alter all the materials but the marshmallow, and "tallest" is defined as the vertical distance between the base of the tower and the top of the marshmallow. With multiple teams the challenge is presented as a competition. There are several lessons to be taken away from the challenge, including those related to collaboration, planning, incentives, and experimentation, and there are many ways to debrief the exercise, depending on which lesson or lessons you wish to highlight. I use the challenge to emphasize my favorite line—delivered by none other than Peter Skillman himself— from the 1999 ABC *Nightline* feature on IDEO in which the design firm had five days to completely rethink and redesign the grocery store shopping cart: "Enlightened trial and error succeeds over the planning of the lone genius."

My reason for giving the black belts this challenge is that I'm fairly confident that I have 40 lone geniuses in the room squinting at me, and I need to drive home Skillman's message. If I fail, they won't embrace design thinking as a profoundly different approach to innovative thinking. I proceed to run the quick 18-minute test.

## THE OVERTHINKING FLAW

*18 minutes on the clock*. I tell them there will be a special prize for the winning team, and they're off. They are highly trained in the discipline of analysis, so I expect a good bit of situational assessment up front. I'm not disappointed. I spy two of the teams counting their sticks of spaghetti, and one team standing the sticks up in order to separate longer sticks from shorter ones. Another team lays their string down on top of the masking tape just to see if they are both the same length, a yard. They're not exactly the same, perhaps a quarter inch discrepancy. Naturally, I get a sharp sideways glare. That quarter inch will make all the difference, I'm sure.

*16 minutes left.* Several of the teams assign roles and divvy up responsibilities, effectively determining how the construction activity will function. They are setting up their organization, but cleverly stop short of drawing an org chart. Discussion on tower infrastructure is in full swing at most tables. All teams have set aside the marshmallow to concentrate on creating a system for erecting a strong and stable structure.

*14 minutes left.* Base and pillar building are in full swing: bases and legs taped to the table top, spaghetti sticks bundled with tape, extended with tape. Most teams go with some sort of triangular structure. Little if any string is used at this point.

*12 minutes left.* Half the teams have erected some sort of free-standing structure and are working on extending the height. The other half are assembling their tower pillars. A few teams are contemplating the string.

*10 minutes left.* Tower structures are up, scaffolding work is in full swing.

*6 minutes left.* No significant change in activity . . . all teams are hard at work, focused on height and stability. Not a lot of discussion is going on, and everyone seems immersed in the task before them.

*3 minutes left.* One team appears ready to crown their tower with a marshmallow. A few more pieces of tape for safe measure and they will be ready. A few teams nearby take notice, realize they need to work quicker to finish their structures, and urge their teammates to hurry. Pressure mounts. The other teams are still working, oblivious to the potential winner.

*2 minutes left.* The one team has a completed marshmallow tower, but it's leaning. They take the marshmallow off and build reinforcements. I give the two-minute warning, just in case they've lost track of the timer on the screen at the front of the room. Nothing is technically freestanding at this point. Realization that the marshmallow is heavier than they thought begins to creep in.

*1 minute left.* Stress is building, even some mild panic. No one wants to be left without a tower. One team has a tower up, so I measure it: 20.5 inches tall.

*Time!* Just the one tower. Three with a marshmallow on top, but requiring a few helping hands. Nine out of ten teams have left the yard of string untouched. Sheepish looks abound, as they realize that the majority failed to complete the basic task of building any kind of marshmallow tower, much less the highest. I declare the winner by default, and bestow the special team prize: the full bag of marshmallows.

"So what happened here?" I ask. I debrief the exercise by focusing on the takeaway lesson I want to deliver by asking them who they think performs the worst on the challenge. More than a few jokingly chime in, "Six Sigma Black Belts!" Close, I tell them. Recent business school graduates is the actual answer. I confess to being a recovering MBA myself. Then I ask them who they think performs best. "Kids!" cry a few. Correct: recent kindergarten school graduates.

The average tower height is 20 inches, according to the research.[9] CEOs, recent MBAs, and attorneys do the worst, collectively falling well short of the 20-inch mark. Kindergarteners, on the other hand, significantly surpass the 20-inch mark, averaging nearly 30 inches. And the reason for this, and what I really want to drive home, is this: kindergarteners build five working prototypes by the time everyone else has executed their one and only attempt near the finish line.

While the children focus quickly on the real problem—the marshmallow—everyone else focuses on the solution, the structure. Unfettered by any special knowledge of geometry, physics, organizational or action planning, children immediately focus on the biggest item in front of them, the marshmallow, and have a freestanding tower up on average inside the five-minute mark. It's not the tallest, but it's up. They then build from there, testing their tower up to four more times, each time making it just a little taller, a little stronger, a little more stable. They tend to use far more of the resources, including the string, pieces of which generally get used as stabilizing guidewires.

Meanwhile, the smart and knowledgeable planners of the world overanalyze and complicate a fairly simple problem, consciously making and often verbalizing the unwarranted assumption that the marshmallow will not present an issue for a strong and stable building. So, they set it aside to spend all their time building around that assumption, essentially ignoring the "freestanding" constraint. Why waste any precious time testing their structure? They are certain their plan will work, so they swing for the fence.

But they are wrong. They have fallen prey to the Overthinking flaw.

## WHY WE OVERTHINK

General George Patton once said, "No plan escapes first contact with the enemy." Ex–heavyweight boxing champ Mike Tyson updated Patton's sentiment by saying, "Everyone has a plan until they get punched in the mouth."

The question is, where did our love of planning come from? Part of the answer comes from our evolutionary addiction to resources:* the more we have, the more we feel safe, secure, in control, shielded from risk, and thus able to perform better. But in reality, just the opposite is often true—the more we attempt to control and regulate apparent risk, the more exposed and at risk we often are. That's because the more protected we think we are, the less vigilant we become.

For example, if you have just had your car fitted with brand-new brakes and tires, your driving behavior will change. Not radically, certainly, but often just enough to invite danger. Because you feel safer and more in control with improved stopping power, you will actually drive a bit faster and brake a bit later, unconsciously converting a set of resources intended to be a safety benefit to what you believe is a performance advantage. On the other hand, if you know your brakes are due for a change and your tires are balding, you'll drive a bit slower and brake a bit sooner, and thus more safely, which is what you were after in the first place. But it

---

* Eons of evolution requiring us to collect and cache supplies needed to survive harsh elements are definitely still part of our genetic imprint: abundant resources still delight us. If you don't believe me, stand outside a Costco or Sam's Club and watch how happy people are as they cart off 48 rolls of toilet tissue.

is not the abundant resources that made you safer, it was the lack of them.

Glance back at the most prevalent and popular solutions given to both the shampoo bottle and videotape challenges, keeping in mind that the constraints in both challenges were that no additional burden could be incurred, and any additional cost must be kept close to nil. Notice that almost all of the solutions offered completely ignore the constraints and require the addition of significant resources. That's another reason I like both the string handcuff and marshmallow challenge: the physical resources are slim and fixed. Just like they are in the real world.

The ability to view finite resources as the very source of creative thought is the hallmark of an artist. As Leonardo da Vinci clearly demonstrated with this tiny masterpiece *Mona Lisa*, it is not the size of the canvas that marks a work of art. Restraining forces always rule, and relying on slack resources or ignoring constraints not only stifles creative thinking, but also breeds Overthinking.

## THE NEUROSCIENCE OF OVERTHINKING

Recall from the previous chapter that it is the quantum Zeno effect that keeps brain regions activated long enough for Hebb's law ("neurons that fire together, wire together") to work. But exactly how does it do this? Through focused attention, referred to as attention density.

*(continued)*

## ATTENTION DENSITY

Attention density makes the quantum Zeno effect "kick in" and causes focused attention to have powerful effects on the brain by activating Hebb's law. The denser your attention is, the more likely a specific habit will be wired into your brain. *Repeatedly* focusing your attention on something strengthens brain circuits, which explains how learning to ride a bike becomes automatic, and why habits are so hard to break.

Here's the thing: attention density cuts both ways, meaning it can work for you or against you. When you focus your attention on a strong and enduring brain circuit, it can slow you down, and even shut you down. Athletes and other performers experience this as *choking*: what has become automatic through years of practice can become crippling under pressure when attention is focused on it.

In other words, thinking too much can indeed be detrimental. In a recent study published in *Nature Neuroscience*,[10] researchers used fMRI to measure brain activity in people as they tapped out six different 10-digit (e.g., 1341244523) sequences on a keyboard, each of which they had practiced hundreds of times over the course of six weeks, until the fastest learners had become so proficient that they were ripping through each set of 10 digits in less than a second.

Results showed that those who learned the sequences faster were also quicker to disengage what we called SLOW thinking in Chapter 2, the deeper thinking we use to tackle complex or unfamiliar challenges and for actively making decisions.

The study authors maintain that your thinking can "get in the way when the information is actually already in your motor memory. If you stop thinking so hard, then you actually perform better." They also stressed that their main finding was a correlation between the ability to disengage from certain cognitive processes and faster learning, not proof that one causes the other.

Colgate University neuroscientist Neil Albert, who was not part of the study, commented that the findings might help explain why children are better than adults at learning a new language. "They can absorb basic building blocks without getting bogged down in analysis. Children don't have the high-level cognitive resources that adults have."

This certainly confirms the results of the marshmallow challenge!

Another part of the answer centers on our need to be certain and correct, a need easily traced to how we learn, and how we are educated. And yes, I am making a distinction between the two.

Consider first the natural learning that occurs long before we ever enter a classroom. By all accounts, it is our most intensive learning period. It features failure upon failure: learning to smile, hold our head up, roll over, grab things, sit up, crawl, walk, talk . . . everything is an experiment, nothing happens right the first time, and what we now call failure was not at that time thought of much less labeled as failure, but rather a continuous cycle of learning and progressing and improving—the very nature of growing.

I remember vividly my daughter as an infant in her high chair dropping food on the floor. She was a perfect little learner, wondering what would happen if she could somehow get her strained carrots on the floor. I'm certain that the problem was somehow framed quite clearly to her—*how do I get them on the ground?*—perhaps not in words, for she could not yet talk. Tracking her eye movements, I watched her consider several hypotheses: she could tip her entire bowl over the tray, she could fill her spoon and flick away, or simply grab a fistful and fling—three viable ways to answer the question.

Now the fun begins. She decides quickly to try the bowl-tip method, and runs her test. Her success metric is obvious: food on the floor. Her test works wonderfully well. In fact, the feedback exceeds her expectations: the noise from her dish as it crashes on the tile gives her great glee, food is everywhere, and Mom gets really busy. Yay! So fun!! It works so well she adopts it as her tentative best practice. As Mom cleans up and replaces a full bowl of food on the tray, she does what any good scientist does, and confirms her results. This time, however, the feedback is a bit different, and not as positive as the initial trial: Mom isn't happy about it, and Dad has to get involved. Lesson learned. So she launches another experiment, this time with the spoon method.

Without any help or guidance, my daughter was learning just fine on her own, in the most powerful way: satisfying her natural curiosity through rapid experimentation. In this type of learning, the test came *before* the lesson. There was no sense of failure, for it was a concept yet to be introduced. Without a sense of failure, she was fearless in her learning and experimenting.

It would not be long before it would disappear. Once in the classroom, her fearless learning through testing was replaced by a new kind of learning. Her teachers now asked the questions, and she had to answer correctly. The need to be certain and correct grew. In a complete reversal of her toddler learning, she faced a new kind of test, one that came *after* the lesson. There was a right and wrong answer involved with this kind of test, and a grade called "F," for failure. Along with grades on tests came fear. As the demands of homework assignments, quizzes, and tests grew, so grew her need to plan her time in order to avoid failure.

By the time she was in third grade, she knew that tests and experiments were different—experiments were reserved for science class. She now knew that "lab" was the "fun" part, something she stopped "real learning" to do. There was learning, and there was experimenting. Different. And wrong.

The good news is that the working world now realizes the errors of our institutions, and is racing to rekindle the childlike ethos of curiosity and experimentation with which we entered the world, eager to embrace what perhaps Charles Kettering said best: "Virtually nothing comes out right the first time. Failures, repeated failures, are finger posts on the road to achievement. The only time you don't want to fail is the last time you try something. One fails toward success."

Which brings us to the third part of the answer to the question of why we Overthink: awareness is a good start, but what we really need is a reliable approach for reuniting learning with experimenting, and reigniting the natural born learner in us. To my mind, all we really have to do is get back in touch with how we made our way in the world those first few formative years.

Kindergarteners doing the marshmallow challenge know the simple secret.

## THE FIX: PROTOTESTING

The remedy for Overthinking is what I call Prototesting, and it is really no different than the one my daughter employed in the high chair, and relearned in science class: question, hypothesize, test, and reflect. Prototesting is mash-up of prototyping and testing. A prototype is defined as an early model of a potential solution that can take many forms, from purely conceptual, like a strategy, to completely physical, like a product. Broadly speaking, though, a prototype in any form is at its core simply a set of educated guesses about the future. And the fancy word for an educated guess is *hypothesis*.* And the purpose of a hypothesis as is to guide a test, an *experiment*. Creating a prototype is play, testing it is *purposeful* play. That's why I like Prototesting as the chosen term for fixing Overthinking—it really captures the essence of the two-step process . . . without overthinking it!

Two powerful tools will help you raise your Prototesting game: The first is a single question for teasing out the assumptions. The second is a simple framework for designing tests of those assumptions. This pair of tools, when taken together and implemented as rapid, iterative loops, creates a formidable Prototesting approach for Overthinking.

---

* Dictionary.com defines hypothesis as: 1. a proposition, or set of propositions, set forth as an explanation for the occurrence of some specified group of phenomena, either asserted merely as a provisional conjecture to guide investigation (working hypothesis) or accepted as highly probable in the light of established facts; 2. a proposition assumed as a premise in an argument. 3. the antecedent of a conditional proposition. 4. a mere assumption or guess.

## Surfacing Assumptions: What Must Be True?

In watching the six sigma folks and hundreds of others engage in the marshmallow challenge, it becomes quite apparent that they think the exercise is just a project, because they leap immediately to project planning and management kinds of activities: assigning roles, doling out resources, aiming for a "one and done" product. But logic dictates that you don't have a project until you have a valid solution to a problem.

Roger Martin, in his seminal book *The Design of Business*, makes a clear distinction between *valid* and *reliable*, writing:

> Many businesses . . . become highly skilled at using algorithms to produce outcomes that are reliable, that is, consistent and predictable. . . . Companies that devote all their resources to reliability lack the tools to pursue outcomes that are valid, that is, that produce a desired result. Indeed, many organizations see no value at all in valid outcomes. Little wonder, then, that those same organizations don't know how to manage validity-seeking activities to generate lasting business value. Advances in knowledge emerge from the pursuit of valid results. That pursuit calls for a different set of tools and processes.[11]

This was certainly evident in the marshmallow challenge that introduced this chapter. Almost to a person the six sigma black belts assumed they already had a valid solution to a problem, and started scaling it up with a reliability-based approach. It was that key assumption that led them astray.

Remember how our mantra begins: *what appears to be the problem, isn't.*

We all make unconscious leaps of faith in our natural enthusiasm and optimistic outlook, but if we want to survive Patton's "first contact with the enemy," and avoid Tyson's getting "punched in the mouth," we must address the assumptions inherent in our potential solutions. If not attended to—teased out, made transparent, and tested—these leaps may indeed become the very blind spots that will put to rest our best-laid plans.

That's why we so often hear that making assumptions is a bad thing.* We don't do a good job of assessing and addressing them. But what we don't know far outweighs what we do, so assumptions are unavoidable. It's how we handle them and exploit them that can make the difference between winning and losing the brain game.

The key lies in the approach. In my experience, trying to list assumptions doesn't work for most people, for a few reasons. First, our assumptions are so ingrained in our thinking and thus so hard to identify—recall what we learned about Fixation in the previous chapter—that it takes a good tool to lend a bit of objectivity. Second, most people tend to list "known" things for the sake of ease and to avoid the risk of looking uncertain. But an assumption by definition is something unknown, untested, a guess. And that's scary . . . we fear the unknown, and we are reticent to bring it up and make it public.

---

* You know, the old quip: when you assume, you make an *ass* of *u* and *me*.

The best technique I've found to surface an assumption and alchemically turn it into an advantage amounts to a single but powerful question: *What must be true?*

I learned this technique from Roger Martin, who's been using it for 20 years, ever since a disappointing consulting engagement in which the client went against his advice, with disastrous results. It was enough to make him reflect on his consultative approach. Then, during a subsequent engagement in which he had a strong view of what the best option for his client would be, he suddenly realized that it didn't matter at all what *he* thought. He realized that what mattered was what *his client* thought, since it would be they who would have to take action one way or the other, not he.

> To surface an assumption and turn it into an advantage, ask:
>     *What Must Be True?*

As Martin tells it: "At an impasse, an idea popped into my head. Rather than have them talk about what they thought *was* true about the various options, I would ask them to specify what would *have to be* true for the option on the table to be a fantastic choice. The result was magical. Clashing views turned into collaboration to really understand the logic of the options. Rather than having people attempt to convince others of the merits of options, the options themselves did the convincing (or failed to do so). In this moment, the best role of the consultant became clear to me: don't attempt to convince clients which choice is best; run a process that enables them to convince themselves."[12]

The goal is not to identify all the many assumptions that may be made, but rather those that are riskiest and most uncertain: your "leaps of faith." Depending on how abstract a given prototype is, there may be several categories worth considering. For example, determining whether a prototype strategy represents a good set of choices may require asking what must be true about the industry structure, market segmentation, distribution channels, cost structures, and competitive reaction. A prototype product or service offering may require asking what must be true about what users truly value.

Once you develop a list of answers to the question of what must be true for your concept to be a good choice, you will have a fairly robust set of conditions for success. This list is your portfolio of educated guesses about the future, your hypotheses. The task becomes one of identifying those that might not be true, and thus represent obstacles and barriers . . . a potential "punch in the mouth."

The easiest and most effective way to do this is to start by asking yourself: Which of the *what must be true?* answers am I most worried might not be true?

In the marshmallow challenge, what might be the most worrisome *what must be true?* Certainly it's that a marshmallow won't topple spaghetti sticks.

It is the most worrisome *what must be true?* that is used to design an initial test.

## Testing Assumptions: Experiment Design

The whole reason for Prototesting is to defeat the Overthinking flaw and increase the likelihood of success, by revealing the assumptions made regarding the future, then constructing experiments to test your thinking. Make no mistake, the assumptions *must* be tested. The goal with Prototesting is to pick the simplest, quickest, cheapest test that is also the most appropriate for the level of abstraction you're dealing with. An initial test of a prototype corporate strategy will look and feel different than, say, an initial test of a marshmallow tower prototype. They will, however, share the primary design elements of all good experiments.

When it comes to test design, I prefer the one offered by Michael Schrage in his book *The Innovator's Hypothesis*. To begin with, I like the way Schrage defines an experiment, because it calls up Roger Martin's notion of validity: "an easily replicable test of a hypothesis that generates meaningful learning and measurable outcomes. It meaningfully and measurably provides some insight into the relationship—if any—between action and outcome. The importance and significance of that insight depends on the design, implementation and interpretation of that simple experiment."[13]

The second thing I like is Schrage's definition of hypothesis: "a testable belief about future value creation." It posits a relationship between an action and an outcome. And in the context of performance, there must be a metric for assessing value. What I like even more is his plug-n-play madlib for constructing a good hypothesis:

**The Team Believes Exploring This [Action/
Capability] Will Likely Result in [Desirable
Outcome], and We'll Know This Because Our
[Metric] [Significantly Changed].**

Finally, Schrage confirms that a prototype is also a hypothesis:

> Prototypes are educated guess about the
> future—the future of how the prototype might
> perform, the future of how potential users
> might react to it, the future of how it might be
> produced or manufactured, the future of how
> people might sell or market it, the future of how
> researchers might explore and test its technical
> features and functionalities further, the future
> of how designers might shape or refine its look
> further, etc. A prototype describes a potential
> future worth testing. A prototype's design
> hypothesis is an assertion of how a design
> choice creates value.[14]

A prototype *is* a hypothesis.

The six-part test design is so simple it needs no further explanation, simply plug in your most worrisome assumption from the What Must Be True? exercise, and you're good to go.

**EXPERIMENT DESIGN TEMPLATE**

| CONDITIONS | |
|---|---|
| Which of our *what must be true?* assumptions are we most worried might not be true? | Why is it so worrisome? |
| **HYPOTHESIS** | |
| What must we learn? | What is our testable belief about future value creation?<br><br>"We believe [action/capability] will likely result in [desired outcome], with [metric] [significantly changed]." |
| **EXPERIMENT** | |
| How will we test our hypothesis? | What is the target metric that will be our standard of proof that helps determine pass/fail? |

"Ride the rapid experimentation learning curve," writes Schrage. "You'll be energized and exhilarated. The more you experiment, the easier it becomes. The easier it becomes, the more you experiment. Virtuous cycles are wonderful. If rapid experimentation doesn't become easier the more you and your colleagues do it, then you're not doing it right. When you're doing it right, the results are remarkable. You can't help but do well."[15]

What is so attractive about Prototesting is that it calls up the kind of learning that creates new and valid knowledge—the kind my daughter engaged in while running her food experiments in the high chair, in which it is the test that produces the lesson.

And the Overthinking flaw fades away.

| TAKEAWAY | The Flaw & The Fix |

## OVERTHINKING

We overthink for several reasons, including an evolutionary addiction to abundant resources and institutional education focused on certainty and reliability in which the test comes after the learning. By reversing this dynamic with simple, fast, and frugal tests of prototypes, we can rekindle the ethos of experimentation young children naturally exhibit, in which the test precedes the learning.

PART TWO

# Mediocre

## CHAPTER 4

# Satisficing

*It's not that I'm so smart, it's just that I stay with problems longer.*

**—ALBERT EINSTEIN**

In Part One we looked at the three most prevalent fatal thinking flaws, and I used a few different thought challenges as the backdrop. They were hard, but we are going to kick it up a notch in Part Two, where we look at the next two thinking flaws—Satisficing and Downgrading—in the context of thinking challenges in which elegant solutions are not as easily achieved, because the challenges themselves are more vexing.

For example, take a look at a more difficult insight problem involving an incorrect Roman numeral equation, like the one I showed you in Chapter 2 (Fixation). In this one, you cannot move or alter in any way either the plus sign or the equals sign. The challenge: Imagine that the numbers are moveable sticks. Leaving the plus and equals signs as they are, what is the least number of sticks you would have to move to correct the equation?*

XI + I = X

---

* In case you forget your Roman numerals, the equation reads, "11 plus 1 equals 10," which is obviously incorrect.

If you answered "one," welcome to Satisficing. I bet you saw a solution right away, in less than a second. Almost everyone does. You probably saw immediately that X + I = XI or IX + I = X are good solutions, right? They are indeed good solutions, but only good enough, because there is a better answer to the original question, which asked about "the least number of sticks" to move. I'm sure you'll agree that an answer of "zero" is the optimal answer, and certainly better than "one." So by employing the Inversion fix, you can recast the problem as "how do I correct the equation without moving any sticks?"

There are three ways. You could simply look at the problem upside down—flipping this book is the easiest way. Or you could get creative and read it literally right to left, so that X (ten) = I (one) plus IX (nine). Or you might recognize the visual symmetry, and reflect it in a mirror. All three ways are different ways to achieve the elegant solution, and involve moving beyond the first obvious solution that looks good enough, which is, by the way, the definition of the fourth fatal flaw, Satisficing.

## THE SATISFICING FLAW

Satisficing is a real word, part satisfying and part sufficing, coined by the late economics Nobel laureate Herbert Simon his 1956 book *Models of Man*. He used it to describe our natural inclination to settle for "good enough" when faced with a decision. In general, we go with the first option that offers an acceptable payoff, choose the one that appears to get us "in the ballpark" quickest, but then stop looking for other ways, including the best way, to solve the problem. We rationalize that the optimal solution is too difficult, not worth the effort involved, or simply unnecessary. Simon called this "bounded rationality."

Forty years after Simon introduced satisficing, MIT lecturer Peter Senge in his book *The Fifth Discipline* wrote, "Business and human endeavors are systems . . . we tend to focus on snapshots of isolated parts of the system. And wonder why our deepest problems never get solved." Senge had it right. Remember the second line of our mantra: *What appears to be the solution, isn't.*

Now, there is a time and place for satisficing, and like many things in life, the secret lies in balance and timing. Satisficing is wonderfully efficient and magically stress-reducing when operating under the appropriate context. In the vast majority of routine, everyday decisions, we'd be wise to satisfice. That's when "good enough" is, well, just that. But when you're trying to solve a difficult problem in which a suboptimal solution could put you at risk is not one of those times.

One of the most common "at risk" contexts is when we are working as part of a larger group—a team, an organization, even a family—for that is where the impact of individual Satisficing can wreak havoc on the interests of other group members. When I begin working with organizations, I often have the teams I'm working with play a game that I call "Win As Much As You Can." It is a simple problem to solve: all you have to do is to decide, as a team, whether you should choose an X or a Y.

Take a look at the rules and scoring:

# WIN AS MUCH AS YOU CAN

## SETTING THE STAGE

Everyone is an associate of The Everyday Organization. You will be divided into four teams. Each team will relocate to one of the four corners of the room.

## THE ASSIGNMENT

Throughout a typical day, decisions are made on a variety of important topics—complex decisions that affect everyone. We're going to make it a lot easier:

- Each team will make a simple decision: Do we choose X or Y?
- We will play 10 rounds. In each round, you will confer with the other members of your team and reach a consensus on your decision.
- You will have 60 seconds in each round to make your decision.
- When you have made your choice, write it (a simple X or Y will do) on a Post-it and hand it to the facilitator.

## PAYOFF SCHEDULE

Sometimes you win, sometimes you lose. In each round, once all decisions have been made and tallied, your team will receive its payoff according to the following schedule. How much will you win?

| 4 X's | Each team loses $10,000 |
|-------|------------------------|
| 3 X's, 1 Y | Each team choosing X wins $10,000<br>The team choosing Y loses $30,000 |
| 2 X's, 2 Y's | Each team choosing X wins $20,000<br>Each team choosing Y loses $20,000 |
| 1 X, 3 Y's | The team choosing X wins $30,000<br>Each team choosing Y loses $10,000 |
| 4 Y's | Each team wins $10,000 |

I've been using this game for nearly 25 years and have played it with hundreds of teams during that time. The results are almost always the same. What happens through the first five rounds is that each team tries to outguess the others, so while the specific mix of X's and Y's varies with each round, no team chooses the optimizing decision: every team chooses Y. I've rarely had a group in which all four teams chose Y during the first half of the game. Smaller teams do not view themselves as part of the larger group, aka The Everyday Organization, and thus do not try to achieve a larger group win. The teams do not communicate with one another, even though I have not expressly prohibited it.

After the fifth round, I have each team select a representative, then have the representatives confer with each other for one minute. The hope here is that by doing this, they will figure out how to make decisions that enable every team to win. I'm hoping that the simple logic of the game is revealed during the short conversation, namely that it is a zero-sum game. Meaning, unless every team chooses Y, someone loses. This is *de facto* suboptimization, and quite possibly the epitome of shortsightedness.

What happens next is nothing short of mind-blowing: *I never get 4 Y's.* In fact, 80 percent of the time an act of outright sabotage occurs, and I field 3 Y's and 1 X. *80 percent of the time!* Then, in the next two rounds, with trust destroyed, teams revert to their original behavior, but the recognition that the higher aspiration is desired is omnipresent. In the eighth round, I have each team select a new representative to confer with the others. With a rare exception or two, rounds nine and ten see all teams choosing Y, thankfully.

But I had to bang them on the head a bit. The Satisficing flaw looms large!

## WHY WE SATISFICE

As I watch people grappling with various thought challenges engage in Satisficing behavior, I see them ignore the very constraints that can paradoxically open up new and different ways of looking at things. I watch them mistakenly pose the question "What should we do?" before asking "What is possible?" They want a solution, but they don't have the patience to pursue the optimal one, favoring implementation over incubation. They would much prefer to throw some resources at the problem and move on, or tweak a previous solution and fit it to the current situation. They fail to look more holistically at the challenge, to search, scan, and see the bigger picture. The result is that elegant solutions completely elude them.

The causes of Satisficing aren't clear, don't enjoy consensus, and run to the complex. Herbert Simon's findings are a start, because they were contrary to what classic economics held at the time, which was that people seek to maximize utility, meaning to get the very best they can from every decision. The problem was that basic economics assumed that people are mostly rational, and armed with complete information regarding their choices. Simon, a behavioral economist, revealed the limitations of maximizing.

"Whereas economic man maximises, selects the best alternative from among all those available to him," he wrote, "his cousin, administrative man, satisfices, looks for a course of action that is satisfactory or 'good enough'." He reasoned that getting all of the information necessary to make the best possible decision was simply too hard. Google wasn't around back then. That didn't deter him, though, because he went on to theorize that the human mind has cognitive limits, such that even if people *could* find all the relevant information easily, they would not be able to process it mentally in any helpful way that informed their pursuits. As he put it, somewhat harshly, "Because he treats the world as rather empty and ignores the interrelatedness of all things (so stupefying to thought and action), administrative man can make decisions with relatively simple rules of thumb that do not make impossible demands upon his capacity for thought."

All of which is to say that lacking a solid algorithm for making decisions, our only choice is to use the most efficient means we have, which are rules of thumb, the fancy name for which is *heuristics*.

## THE POWER OF HEURISTICS

Imagine you're a contestant on the old *Let's Make a Deal* game show. Host Monty Hall offers you the chance to win a new car. It's behind one of three closed doors. Behind each of the other two, however, is a goat.*

You choose a door, and Monty, who knows where the car is, of course, opens one of the remaining two doors to reveal a goat. He offers you a choice: stay where you are, or switch to the other closed door.

*Do you stay with your choice, or switch?*

When I give this thought challenge in workshops, most people stay with their choice. When I ask why, the answer comes quickly: "Two doors left, 50-50 chance, why switch?" When I ask people who say they would switch what their reasoning was, the answer is the same: "Two doors left, 50-50 shot, why not switch?"

That is a heuristic in action. "50-50" is a rule of thumb meaning equal odds. But, "stay" is a satisficing move. "Switch" is a maximizing move, and the winning one. The heuristic led you astray in this case.

*Always switch!*

---

* In September 1991 a reader of Marilyn vos Savant's column in the *New York Times* magazine *Parade* posed this very question, now known as the Monty Hall Problem, with its own Wikipedia entry. She answered correctly that the contestant should switch doors. Her answer provoked nearly 10,000 responses from readers, most of them disagreeing with her. Several were from mathematicians and scientists whose responses lamented the nation's lack of math skills, and who later had to retract their statements. I first wrote about the Monty Hall Problem a decade ago in *The Elegant Solution*.

There are only two scenarios, stay and switch. Each has three possibilities. Here's how it works. Let's say you pick door #1. Monty opens any door without a car behind it. If you run through each three-door possibility in the "Stay" and "Switch" scenarios, the spread looks like this:

| DOOR 1 | DOOR 2 | DOOR 3 | STAY WITH DOOR 1 | SWITCH |
|--------|--------|--------|------------------|--------|
| **CAR** | Goat | Goat | **WIN** | LOSE |
| Goat | **CAR** | Goat | LOSE | **WIN** |
| Goat | Goat | **CAR** | LOSE | **WIN** |

*You have twice the odds of winning if you switch!*

The role of host Monty Hall is the key. Remember, Monty will always show you a goat door before asking you to stay or switch. So while your heuristic says *two doors, 50-50 shot, stay put*—thinking a bit more like a maximizer will produce the win you want.

But we now live in a Google world, and information is massively abundant, so much so that too much information can exhaust our attention and loop us into an Overthinking mode, where too many choices not only stall our progress, but can actually make us unhappy. Swarthmore College professor and psychologist Barry Schwartz, author of *The Paradox of Choice: Why Less Is More*, in a follow-up study to his famous research[16] on people facing 24 varieties of jam, followed over 500 job-seeking college seniors at several different colleges for the eight months leading up to their graduation. The results were confirming: the maximizers landed better jobs, with starting salaries on average 20 percent higher than those of the satisficers, but they felt worse about their jobs. And a recent study[17] underscored the finding, by showing that not only were satisficers more satisfied after making an irreversible decision, but given the choice of irreversibility or reversibility in a future decision, they would prefer it to be irreversible, presumably to avoid needless worry or second-guessing. Maximizers, as you can imagine, were more satisfied after making a reversible decision, and would prefer reversibility if they had the option in a future decision, presumably to avoid what we now call FOMO: Fear of Missing Out.

At this point, you may see the similarities between Leaping and Satisficing when it comes to the deeper thinking required to address tougher challenges: both call up the wrong thinking at the wrong time. In other words, Satisficing is a perfectly sound strategy for picking jams and even jobs, but when faced with higher-order decisions or seeking farther-reaching solutions in which the potential impact can result in significant downstream effects that prevent us from achieving the kind of success we seek, we need to give the pursuit of an optimal solution more consideration. We need to wear the hat of the maximizer if we want to win.

First century philosopher Epictetus gives us a clue to the fix for Satisficing (in those situations in which we would be better off maximizing) saying: "In every affair consider what precedes and follows, and then undertake it. Otherwise you will begin with spirit; but not having thought of the consequences, when some of them appear you will shamefully desist."

Meaning, action isn't bad, as long as you've given careful thought to what it is you really want.

## THE FIX: SYNTHESIS

Herbert Simon also introduced the world to the concept of *design thinking* in his 1969 book *The Sciences of the Artificial*, making a strong case for the importance of designers to pursue alternative solutions, writing: ". . . problem-solving systems and design procedures in the real world do not merely assemble problem solutions from components but must search for appropriate assemblies. In carrying out such a search, it is often efficient to divide one's eggs among a number of baskets—that is, not to follow out one line until it succeeds completely or fails definitely but to begin to explore several tentative paths, continuing to pursue a few that look most promising at a given moment. If one of the active paths begins to look less promising, it may be replaced by another that had previously been assigned a lower priority."[18]

Simon is talking about the fix for Satisficing in the context of problem-solving: Synthesis. An easy way to think about Synthesis is "both-and" thinking, versus the kind of thinking both Simon and Barry Schwartz were studying, which was "either-or." Synthesis lies at the core of Roger Martin's *integrative thinking*, which is the basis for both his 2009 book *The Opposable Mind* as well as the foundation for University of Toronto's graduate business program at the progressive Rotman School of Management, which is focused on developing successful leaders who "rather than accepting the unattractive trade-offs the world presents them, see it as their job to overcome the trade-off and build a new and better model that resolves it and creates new value for world."[19]

Consider the challenge facing Piers Handling, who in 1994 became director of the Toronto International Film

Festival.[20] Before coming under Handling's management, the festival did not enjoy the level of prestige it does today, and certainly nowhere near that of the famous Cannes Film Festival. At the time, it was called Festival of Festivals, open to the public, and focused on Toronto's local film industry and movie-lovers. This approach lacked the status and appeal that invitation-only Cannes had to the broader industry, including film producers and celebrities, who were attracted to the exclusivity absent in the Toronto model. As Handling saw it, switching to the Cannes approach would entail an unacceptable trade-off: alienating the robust Toronto industry and audience. He saw that the tension between inclusivity and exclusivity could not be easily resolved with a simple mashing together of the two opposing models.

Handling looked to synthesize a solution that appealed to every interested party. He thought about what mattered most to the various players: celebrities seeking publicity for their movies, moviegoers rubbing elbows with movie stars, news media seeking stories; production studios seeking box office success; event marketers wanting broad audience exposure. What Toronto had going for it was the massive movie audience, which was a good proxy for the larger North American market.

He examined the ingredients of the Cannes formula and found that the real draw for industry insiders was the enormous media buzz around the prestigious grand prize—the Palme d'Or. He realized that winning the award, though, was not an indicator of eventual box office success. Box office success is a matter of audience preference, not industry preference. That was Handling's *Aha!* moment.

Enter the People's Choice Award, which at the time was a small award buried in the Toronto Film Festival agenda. The People's Choice is decided not by a select jury like the Palme d'Or, but by moviegoers . . . the people who spend money and actually determine a film's financial success. Handling recast the People's Choice Award as the highlight of the festival. It was a brilliant synthesis, blending the best of what Cannes had to offer in terms of industry appeal and buzz with Toronto's best feature: its audience.

Today, the Toronto International Film Festival is one of the most prestigious events of its kind in the world, and, according to *Variety*, "second only to Cannes in terms of high-profile pics, stars and market activity."[21]

Roger Martin and Jennifer Riel suggest that "by following the example of integrative thinkers like Piers Handling," we can learn to take a more sophisticated and rigorous approach to thinking, and offer two Synthesis techniques.[22]

## 2 Ways to Synthesize

### 1. Double Down

This is what Piers Handling did in rethinking the Toronto International Film Festival. You have two solutions, one of which has many benefits with one huge drawback and the other of which has one huge benefit but many drawbacks. Taking a cue from Blackjack players who double down on a hot hand may be a way to synthesize a third option. Martin and Riel state that, "The trick is to find the conditions under which the first model can produce the benefits of the second." They give the example of Walmart, facing a huge drawback in the form of a massive erosion of their global reputation if they did not change both their stance on environmental sustainability as well as carbon footprint. Doing so would be expensive, which for a low-cost provider strategy is a big drawback, but would do wonders for the company's reputation. Walmart effectively doubled down by extending their general strategy of placing pressure on suppliers to reduce costs. In this case they placed pressure on their suppliers to adopt more environmentally friendly strategies, refusing to purchase goods from suppliers who did not meet certain standards for water, waste, and carbon. As Martin and Riel write, "In short, Walmart extended its business-as-usual model in order to produce a reputation for environmental leadership. The essential question to ask in this scenario: Under what conditions could model A actually generate the benefits of model B?"

### 2. Decomposition.

When you have two equally attractive solutions that you wish you could fully implement simultaneously but can't because they are in direct conflict and require significant trade-offs, break the larger context down into component parts, so that you can apply each solution in whole to those components. For example, when Target was in its early years, its senior executives realized they faced a dilemma: it had to contend on one hand with Walmart, far and away the low-cost retail leader. Seeing Kmart relegated to also-ran status, Target knew it couldn't win the game of everyday items offered at rock-bottom prices. On the other hand, it faced successful, highly differentiated department store retailers, such as Nordstrom and Macy's, strong brands that would be nearly impossible to steal significant share from, much less unseat. In order to compete effectively, Target adopted a strategy of decomposition. It decided that groceries and everyday commodities—a box of Tide, a package of Bounty—would be sold at prices equivalent to Walmart's. However, when it came to apparel and other higher-margin items, Target chose to partner with well-known designers and celebrity homemakers looking for broader audiences. These offers had no direct substitutes at either Walmart or higher end retailers, and Target was able to create the illusion of being a discounter in one part of the store, and a unique retailer in another. It broke the problem down and essentially created two stores under one roof, becoming a discounter-plus-retailer, convincing people that they could get fashionable things along with the halo of everyday low prices from the store within a store. It worked. Target grew exponentially, carving out a unique playing field on which it could win.*

As with all Synthesizing, the goal of decomposition is to avoid satisficing compromises and "either-or" trade-offs in order to create more value through "both-and" thinking. As Martin and Riel write, "Rather than choosing Option A or Option B to apply to the entire situation, or at all times, the integrative thinker applies the different models together by carefully distinguishing when and how each model can be applied to which elements of the problem space. Each model is then applied selectively. The essential question to ask in

---

* Roger Martin told this story of Target to me and a team of executives in a joint client strategy session held in Santa Monica, California, December 1, 2015.

this scenario: Can I parse the problem in a new way, such that I can apply each model to a different part of the problem space?"

Now, one of the practical challenges in becoming a more integrative thinker is that problems requiring a more sophisticated, Synthesis approach don't come along quite as often as much as other, less difficult problems, so we don't have as many opportunities to practice and develop our Synthesis skills. I have a rather outside-the-box remedy: enter cartoon caption contests, like the most famous one offered weekly by the *New Yorker*, or the one offered monthly (with a distinctly business orientation) by *Harvard Business Review*.[23]

## PRACTICING THE ART OF SYNTHESIS

### (Or How to Win the *New Yorker* Cartoon Caption Contest)

Would you attempt solve a problem in which your chances of winning are less than 10,000:1? The *New Yorker* cartoon editor Robert Mankoff wrote in 2010 that "So far there have been 1,449,697 entries and 254 winners. So, roughly, that puts the odds at 10,000:1."

I didn't mind those odds, and solved the problem of winning the contest, using a bit of synthesis.* And I'm not the least bit funny, according to my wife.

---

* My winning caption appeared in the March 24, 2008, print edition of the *New Yorker*.

I do, however, tend to the maximizer side, preferring to exhaust my best thinking. I've observed too many creative sessions in which participants hit a brick wall, satisfice, select obvious ideas, and end up with tired, me-too, ho-hum solutions.

"Good enough" thinking won't win the *New Yorker* contest, because unlike other problems, you have no opportunity to sell people on the benefits of your solution. It must stand on its own.

What the *New Yorker* contest cartoons do so very well is to present you with two opposing or incongruent ideas and challenge you to resolve them. It is a synthesis challenge *par excellence*.

Rather than wait for a sudden flash of creative humor, which is just wishful thinking, I employed integrative thinking. The synthesis began with considering the captionless panel, which showed a couple in bed wearing hazardous material suits, with the partners turned toward each other, apparently having some sort of exchange.

*(continued)*

I first listed word tags related to the context: bed, motel, sex, etc. Note that stopping here would only result in a satisficial caption, one far too obvious to win. I then listed word tags related to the extreme anomaly of the hazmat suits: protection, suit, hazardous, personal space, overkill, sickness, etc.

Only then did I begin the process of meshing and mashing, generating a number of possibilities. The one I liked the most was the simplest: "Next time can we just get flu shots like everyone else?" The other two finalists focused on the obvious: sex. In other words, they satisficed. Good enough to place, but not good enough to win.

I am not bragging. I am merely trying to point out the power of integrative thinking and Synthesis, and how it can help you win the brain game.

Consider incorporating the *New Yorker* weekly contest as a regular bit of integrative thinking practice. As Bob Mankoff says, you have to play (a lot) to win.

I will leave this chapter with the wisdom of Roger Martin:

> Most of us, most of the time, do whatever we can to simplify this [problem-solving] process: we cut down the number of variables we will consider to a minimum; we think about the simplest and most straightforward kinds of causal relationships; we break the problem apart into manageable chunks and then accept the trade-offs that emerge from our thinking as "inevitable." Or, we imagine the trade-offs

away . . . taking the shortest possible route to remedying the tension between the two models. We do all of this in a highly implicit way, failing to look deeply into our thinking at each stage, and thus when we fall victim to a logical misstep, we are entirely unaware of it and only become cognizant of a problem when the outcome is not what we would wish for ourselves.

Integrative thinkers show us what is possible: they consider more features of the problem as salient to its resolution; they consider more complex kinds of causal relationship between the features; they are able to keep the whole problem in mind while they work on the individual parts; and they end up with creative resolutions. Importantly, they do all of this *explicitly*, pushing to understand "the thinking behind their thinking."[24]

---

**TAKEAWAY**   The Flaw & The Fix

### SATISFICING

We satisfice for a variety of reasons, most of them focused on our bias for action and emphasis on short-term expediency and efficiency. By taking a more maximizing approach to complex problems that entails examining various options before synthesizing a solution that incorporates the best of multiple worlds, we can achieve longer-term effectiveness and sustainable success.

## CHAPTER 5

# Downgrading

*One should not pursue goals that are easily achieved.*
*One must develop an instinct for what one can just*
*barely achieve through one's greatest efforts.*

**—ALBERT EINSTEIN**

**S**cene: *10:30 a.m., Parramatta Westfield, Sydney, Australia, April 27, 1983.* As the 10 professional ultramarathon runners lined up for the first ever 875-kilometer (542.5-mile) Westfield Ultramarathon from Sydney to Melbourne, an eleventh man approached the starting line, looking clearly out of place. He appeared to be much older than the other men, twice the age of some, and his threadbare attire was nowhere near as fancy as the fine Nike and Adidas running gear the others were sporting. His varicose veins embarrassed him, so instead of runners' shorts, he wore long plastic track pants to cover them. The pants had a series of small scissor-cut holes in them so he wouldn't overheat under the Australian sun. While the other contestants had several different pairs of running shoes, he had a single well-worn pair that didn't look capable of lasting 875 kilometers. He didn't have sponsors, like all the other racers, nor a large support team or a mobile home to sleep in during the week long race. He looked like just some old guy lingering, loitering, and lumbering about.

But he wasn't. He was racing. His name was Cliff Young, a 61-year-old potato farmer from "out Beech Forest way" who, in the press buildup to the event, had become known for his rather peculiar running background: chasing livestock around the family farm in waders and gumboots because he did not own a horse. He ran with an awkward style more like an erratic, slow shuffle than a runner's smooth stride. As biographer Julietta Jameson put it, "To anyone seeing it for the first time, Cliffy's shuffle might have looked like it would never get anyone anywhere, let alone get a bloke from Sydney to Melbourne. And if it did, it couldn't possibly get a person that distance quicker than blokes with gaits honed by specialist training and sports science."[25]

He was indeed an amateur compared to the rest of the field, all of whom were highly trained, elite athletes with deep marathon experience, winning records, and expert knowledge of how to run a race. He took his false teeth out because they rattled too loudly when he ran. By all measures, he was far more novelty than serious threat. When the starting gun went off he was left in the dust, just as everyone expected, in a true *Tortoise and Hare* kind of way.

Conventional ultramarathon wisdom held that runners should run 18 hours and sleep 6. Cliff Young did not know that, and no one told him. He had no idea of what it took to win a multiday race 875 kilometers long. In fact, he wasn't entirely sure of the route, and took a wrong turn on the first day. Since he didn't know about the 18-hour "limit," while the other competitors retired for the evening, Cliff Young just kept going. Even when a cold rain began to fall, he kept going. When he finally stopped to rest at midnight, he had gone over 100 kilometers without food.

As he started off on his second day, he did not know that his alarm clock had gone off two hours early, and simply began running. And he kept running, in that slow, awkward shuffle. After the second day, he slept for a single hour, and kept running. He continued in that pattern, not knowing what smart ultramarathoners know, that you are supposed to sleep for six hours, that the body has its limits. Henry Ford, who once said, "It has been my observation that most people get ahead during the time that others waste," would have been proud.

Whatever Cliff Young lacked in talent and experience, he more than made up for in mental toughness and grit. Perhaps the old maxim of where there's a will there's a way is true, because in a magnificent display of mind over matter, Cliff Young won the race on the fifth day, finishing a full ten hours ahead of the second place competitor, who knew, of course, what every expert ultramarathoner knows, that you can't run 875 kilometers in five days, 14 hours, and 35 minutes—the equivalent of almost four marathons a day, without six hours of sleep each night.*

You certainly can't if your brain leans toward Downgrading.

## THE DOWNGRADING FLAW

Henry Ford once said, "If you think you can or can't, you're right." In that single line he captured the sum and substance

---

* I heard the Cliff Young story several times from the late Lou Tice, founder of the Pacific Institute, who was a frequent visitor to the University of Toyota during my early tenure there in the late 1990s.

of Downgrading. Cliff Young did not know that the whole world thought that running the Westfield Ultramarathon in the manner he did could not be done, so he was not limited by that mental constraint. In fact, his naïveté in all likelihood enabled him to win in the manner he did—because he didn't know it "couldn't be done," he was empowered to do it. Downgrading does not exist without a mental limit. It exists *because* of a mental limit.

Downgrading is much like Satisficing, but is more of a premeditated, downward or backward revision of a stated goal. Downgrading, if left unchecked, often results in total disengagement from the challenge, a complete abandonment of objectives. The problem you're trying to solve remains unsolved.

Downgrading manifests itself in several ways. In the Prisoner's Release (rope handcuff) challenge, for example, it takes but a few seconds for participants to begin parsing the instructions stating that the handcuffs may not leave your hands at any time. In a true revisionist manner, they'll reinterpret "your" to mean "our" and transfer one set of handcuffs to their partner and triumphantly sing out, "Ta-Da!"

In the shampoo and videotape challenges, the constraints are either completely ignored or immediately revised, the outcome being ideas that clearly fall well short of the admittedly stretch but achievable goals—0 percent theft or 100 percent customer rewind—followed by the selection and selling of an inferior solution. Or the trusty *Pareto* (80-20 rule) solution: "You won't stop people from stealing the shampoo completely, but we can stop 80 percent of it with our solution." They will proceed to rationalize away the other constraints with rhetoric intended to render them irrelevant.

The paradox at play here is that by Downgrading we somehow fool ourselves into believing we can declare victory . . . through a preemptive surrender! I see this happen often in project teams, and I call it "gaming the goal." The legendary Jack Welch faced this very issue during his tenure as CEO of General Electric. Welch was known for his winner's mindset, demanding that all GE lines of business maintain no less than second place in market share, and preferably first. But his lieutenants began gaming the goal by revising how they defined their respective markets, shrinking the market small enough that they could declare themselves number one or two in the space. Welch caught on, though, and reset the constraint so that no business could hold more than a 10 percent share, believing that if people defined their market to be much larger than their share of it, they would be more aggressive in pursuing opportunities to win the top spot.[26]

Psychologist Eric Klinger described the Downgrading process nearly 40 years ago, calling it the *incentive-disengagement cycle*.[27] When we view a problem as unsolvable or a goal as unattainable, we go through four phases. The first thing we do is try harder. No surprise there. Next, if our efforts don't yield the results we want, we get angry. Again, no surprise . . . happens every time I double fault my tennis serve. Third, we resign, mentally distancing ourselves from the goal, and we get depressed. Finally, our commitment dissolves completely and we become open to committing to a new goal. I'm fairly certain all of the world goes through these four phases each year with their high-spun New Year's resolutions, and do so before January ends. As you will discover by the end of the chapter, though, there is new research on just how to exploit this cycle to defeat the Downgrading flaw.

A recent study by researchers at University of Zurich and University of Berne[28] looked at marathon runners, not unlike those racing against Cliff Young, and introduced a concept they call an *action crisis*. "An action crisis," they write, "is conceptualized as a situation in which individuals have already invested a great deal into their goal, but suffer repeated setbacks and/or a substantial loss in the perceived desirability of the goal, and thus become caught between further goal pursuit and disengagement from the goal, asking themselves whether to stop or go." By following a group of marathon runners, some of whom suffered such an action crisis, they discovered a "mindset shift" in which the runners consciously devalue their goal of completing the marathon.

In other words, they Downgrade. The question is why?

## WHY WE DOWNGRADE

Perhaps one explanation for Downgrading is that it comes naturally, and perhaps too easily. How often do we unconsciously sell short our capability? Let's try a quick exercise:

1. Stand up, feet planted shoulder width apart, arms straight out at your sides, elbows locked, in the "Vitruvian Man" pose.
2. Twist your torso all the way to the right as far as you possibly can go.
3. Sight down your right arm and mentally mark your stopping point on the wall, where the tips of

your fingers stop. Remember that mark using some visual clues.

4. Turn back around to face front. Read the next step.
5. Close your eyes and repeat the exercise, stopping when you think you've met your previous stopping point. THEN . . . go just a little past it. Open your eyes when you're done.

Did you surpass your first mark? When I do this in seminars, almost everyone does. My point is that we often and automatically impose limits on ourselves that can unnecessarily hold us back, rather than propel us forward. The fact is that we can't possibly know our true limits until we put our capacity on trial.

I have recently taken to timing how long it takes for participants in the Prisoner's Release challenge to ask out loud, "Is this really possible?" In a sample size of roughly 500 people, the average time is 43 seconds. I make it a point to assure them that it is, and that I am not an evil facilitator. I cheerfully remind them about the third leg of our motto: *what appears to be impossible, isn't.*

The question, "Is this really possible?" is by no means an unreasonable one. In fact, I'm sure it's a sign of rationality, or at least sanity. Interestingly, though, once answered, people go back to doing exactly what they were doing before, expecting different results, which hints at Albert Einstein's definition of insanity.

Fourteen hundred engineers cried a collective "Impossible!" when in 1983 Toyota leadership announced the goal of producing a luxury performance sedan that would beat the best Mercedes and BMW in every possible measure. It took just six years, essentially starting from scratch, but the first Lexus did just that.*

Southwest Airlines employees, along with competitors, aircraft manufacturers, and even Federal Aviation Administration officials collectively cried "Impossible!" when the company's senior leadership set a goal of 10-minute gate turns, which were eventually accomplished by adapting the techniques used by Formula One pit crews.

When the general manager of Toyota's parts distribution business unit set a three-year goal to simultaneously save $100 million in costs, eliminate $100 million in inventory, and improve customer satisfaction 50 percent, her 80 lieutenants collectively cried "Impossible!" But the manager held her ground, and 10 supporting goals were set. While the actual results fell a bit short—$90 million in inventory and a 35 percent bump in satisfaction—she knew they would not have been achieved had she set her sights lower.

The entire Mars Pathfinder team at NASA's Jet Propulsion Laboratory cried a collective "Impossible!" when NASA gave them three years and $150 million to land a rover on Mars, but they did it.

Yes, these are cherry-picked examples; the important point is that in each case, the required capabilities were either present or acquired or developed, and what I call *dramatic destinations* set by the leaders of the respective organizations were audacious and arduous, but informed and intelligent, and so drove radically different thinking.

---

* Engineers from a competing manufacturer dismantled two early Lexus LS400 cars, and concluded that they could not be built, at least not by them.

But the question speaks to another reason we Downgrade, which is the lack of an appropriate challenge. As we discovered in Part One there is an art to framing any challenge. What we did not discuss, however, was the capability to produce what will eventually fill the frame: the solution. You can have the most beautiful picture frame in the world, but if you're aiming for a masterpiece and your ability to paint is as lacking as mine, you're in for disappointment. In other words, a goal must be achievable, a problem solvable. Otherwise, we will disconnect. It's fair game to articulate an audacious goal for yourself, as long as you either have or can acquire or develop the means to achieve it.*

## THE NEUROSCIENCE OF GOAL-DIRECTED ACTION

### The Motive and the Means

"Actions are constituted by both movement and mind," write the authors of a study at UCLA that examined goal hierarchy.[29] "Actions possess both a *how*—the executed movements of the body and its mechanical interactions with the physical world around it—and a *why*—the relatively disembodied motives, beliefs, and intentions of the actor."

*(continued)*

---

* I'm often asked about the Lexus tagline, which refers to the pursuit of perfection, mostly because I maintain that perfection is not achievable. If perfection is not achievable, I'm asked, why pursue it? The answer is that perfection is in fact not the goal, but rather a vector, like the horizon line. Perfection as a pursuit and process drives breakthroughs. Perfection as a goal can stall progress and stunt creativity.

The researchers used functional magnetic resonance imaging (fMRI) to scan and record the brain activity of subjects as they wore video goggles to view videos of people performing routine activities, such as browsing the web, lifting weights, and brushing their teeth. Participants were asked both *how* and *why* people typically perform each action. For the *how* questions, the participants were told to think of one necessary part of performing the action; for the *why* questions, they were told to think of one plausible motive for performing the action.

Here's the thing: the *how* and the *why* lit up completely different parts of the brain: *how* thinking engaged the left brain circuitry, while *why* thinking engaged right brain circuitry. The findings also suggest an inverse relation between the two circuits, meaning when one is on the other is off.

The implications are significant: a well-structured goal requires a *how* as well as a *why* for whole-brain engagement, and it is important to maintain a connection between both. However, trying to focus on both simultaneously may work against us. (See *Fix* section for further tips.)

Another possible reason for Downgrading is the lack of perseverance and passion for long-term goals, or as University of Pennsylvania psychology researcher Angela Duckworth calls it, *grit*.

Duckworth's 2004 study of West Point cadets as they progressed through a brutal first summer initiation training called "Beast Barracks" focused on this very issue.[30] "Beast

Barracks is deliberately engineered to test the very limits of cadets' physical, emotional, and mental capacities," the study reads. Roughly 60 of the some 1,200 or so freshman cadets drop out during the Beast Barracks summer. "A reasonable response to the unrelenting dawn-to-midnight trials of Beast Barracks would be to exchange the goal of graduating from West Point for a more manageable goal such as graduating from a liberal arts college."

In other words, Downgrading was a very real possibility.

Duckworth expected grit, as measured by her proprietary 12-question Grit Scale, to predict cadet retention through Beast Barracks better than could either IQ or a summary measure of cadet quality used by the West Point admissions committee. Results confirmed her hypothesis: "Grit predicted completion of the rigorous summer training program better than any other predictor." The grittier the cadet, the more likely they were to make it through Beast Barracks.

The concept of grit indeed captures the essence of the study's opening quote, taken from psychology pioneer William James's 1907 book, *Pragmatism: A New Name for Some Old Ways of Thinking*:

> Compared with what we ought to be, we are only half awake. Our fires are damped, our drafts are checked. We are making use of only a small part of our possible mental resources . . . men the world over possess amounts of resource, which only exceptional individuals push to their extremes of use.

It seems Downgrading is nothing new.

## THE FIX: JUMPSTARTING

Jumpstarting is my term for tapping into alternate sources of thinking power that help to revitalize and rejuvenate the creative neurons that may be blocking us from pursuing what seems to be impossible, but almost never truly is.

It is beyond the scope of this book to discuss the ins and outs, pros and cons of what the business world calls "stretch goals," a term many attribute to Jack Welch. Stretch goals are widely covered in both popular and academic literature.* It's great fun to talk about them in retrospect, as I have, when they produce breakthrough thinking. My only rule of thumb when it comes to crafting challenges is to use the *Why? What if? How?* questions we discussed in Chapter 1 to first tell yourself a happy story of what your world looks like in the future if your problem goes away entirely, then working backward (how did you go about solving it?) to ensure that story gets told.

This is the "instinct for what one can just barely achieve through one's greatest efforts" that Albert Einstein was referring to in the opening quote of this chapter. And this, more than anything, will help you think about your winning aspiration . . . and winning is the aim of this book. This much I know to be true: if you don't set out to win—however you

---

* Many such treatments are biased pro or con, and almost always conflate cause and effect. The most balanced study on stretch goals in organizations that I've found was led by Sim Sitkin of Duke University: "The Paradox of Stretch Goals: Organizations in Pursuit of the Seemingly Impossible," *Academy of Management Review*, 2011, Vol. 36, No. 3, pp. 544–556. The study concluded that organizations most likely to benefit from stretch goals are least likely to use them, while those least likely to benefit from them are the most likely to use them.

define it—you most certainly will not think about how to do so. And if you're not thinking about winning, you won't take action in that direction.

In other words, as long as you're chasing a challenge that *seems* impossible, I'm much more interested in the nature of your progress toward thinking through it, and in helping you stick to whatever ambitious track you're on when you find your mental energy waning and in danger of Downgrading.

Enter Jumpstarting, which Google's dictionary defines both as "starting a stalled vehicle whose battery is drained by connecting it to another source of power" and "giving an added impetus to something that is proceeding slowly or is at a standstill." I view Jumpstarting as a three-gear battery recharger, employing three effective methods I've used with both teams and individuals, including myself, in order to avoid Downgrading and eventual disengagement.

## Can-If Cascading

During my tenure with University of Toyota, I was involved in a rebranding effort of the Lexus brand. Lexus retained noted brand strategist Adam Morgan, coauthor of *A Beautiful Constraint*, to help guide the effort. One of Morgan's techniques, called "Can-If," a close cousin to *What if?*, has become a favorite of mine. If the first reaction to a challenge (even a private one of your own) is some version of "Impossible!" you've probably set a worthy goal. But emotional reactions like "Impossible!" can quickly decay into rational ones that start with "I/we can't because . . ." It's a very slippery slope, because before you know it, you've completely talked yourself out of a winning aspiration.

That's where "Can-If" comes in. The concept is quite simple: force yourself to replace "can't, because" with a "can, if" statement. If you're on the Mars Pathfinder team, for example, "We can't land a rover on Mars for $150 million, because landing modules cost too much" might become "We can land a rover on Mars if we figure out a way to land without a landing module." You then keep going, using either another *Can-If* or, if a single *Can-If* does the trick, a Framestorming *What if?* or *How?* You never know, you might come up with the elegant solution the Pathfinder team did: use air bags like those found in automobiles to bounce the rover to a stop on Mars.

"Without a positive construct," says Morgan, "the inability to have a ready answer to a difficult question kills the momentum and the flow of exploration."

Converting a "Can't-Because" to a "Can-If" is just such a positive construct, as it is an effective way to Jumpstart the effort, and to keep it rolling once you're on your way.

## Why-How Laddering

From neuroscience we know that both a *why* and a *how* must be present and connected to keep us engaged in the pursuit of a challenge. The first is about purpose, the second is about process. And since we know that focusing on both *why* and *how* isn't possible, we need a practical method to call one or the other up when we begin to stall and contemplate Downgrading. Seemingly impossible challenges seem impossible because there is no clear *how*, and the entire point of such a challenge is the creative search for a solution. So we can be fairly confident that we are in for a difficult struggle with the *how* at some point.

That's where *Why-How Laddering* comes in. If the *how* isn't yielding the desired progress, we can ladder up to asking ourselves the *why*. If the *why* isn't as clear as it could be, we can ladder down to a lower level *how* until we find something we can accomplish to get a quick win and restart our progress toward the *why*.

One of my favorite Jumpstarting stories entailing this kind of laddering comes from Marcus Buckingham, concerning the turnaround of the ailing British prison system.[31] When Sir David Ramsbotham retired from the esteemed position of adjutant general of the British Army in 1993 and was appointed Her Majesty's Chief Inspector of Prisons for England and Wales, he inherited a system in a tailspin. Since Sir David's latitude to effect change was limited to inspection, he couldn't very well go in and tell the heads of prisons to change their ways. Instead, he had to make things happen by changing things within his domain of control: inspection. He chose to focus on the goal of the British prison system, and the measure of success against which prisons were inspected. As you would expect, the *why* of the prison system at the time was to prevent escape, and the logical measure of success was the number of escapees. But as he began to think about the problem, he concluded that the main *why* of a prison system should not be keeping prisoners off the streets, but rather to make sure they didn't come back once released. The new *why* meant a new metric: number of repeat offenders. This new *why* effectively turned the prison system upside down. Sir David challenged the management teams of each prison to significantly shift their focus and to devote their energies toward figuring out new *hows:* processes and programs specifically designed to rehabilitate the prisoners while they were incarcerated, and better ways to ease them back into society once they were released.

## Fresh Starts

The "Fresh Start Effect" is the term University of Pennsylvania professor Katherine Milkman uses in her recent study[32] of the same name to describe the feeling we get when the new year hits and we fire up to set aggressive goals for the coming 12 months. According to the study, people are more likely to set a new goal corresponding with or immediately following an event such as a birthday or the start of a week, month, season, or year, suggesting that temporal landmarks or timestamps might make it easier to engage in aspirational behavior.

For example, the researchers asked hundreds of participants to describe a goal they wished to achieve. After describing the goal, participants were offered a courtesy reminder several months hence as an encouragement to pursue their goal. Half the group was offered a reminder date of "March 20, the third Thursday in March," while the other half was offered "March 20, the first day of spring." More people chose the latter date, which signaled the start of a new cycle.

Milkman proposes two mental processes to explain the effect. First, that these landmarks create new "mental accounting periods" that psychologically distance our present self from its past imperfections, propelling us to behave in line with their renewed self. Second, temporal landmarks interrupt attention to day-to-day details, causing us to take a big-picture view of our situation and focus more on the broader challenge we're chasing.

But you do not need to wait for the new year, your next birthday, or even Monday morning. The Fresh Start effect is something I've been using for several years now (without calling it that), having learned from author and The Energy Project CEO Tony Schwartz about the power of *pulsing*: working in 90-minute cycles, effectively achieving the Fresh Start effect several times a day. It doesn't matter much what you do as long as you change your space every 90 minutes or so. You'll be surprised at the reenergizing effect this has on you. I do it now out of habit and ritual, even when I think I don't need it.

We've known for decades that not only do we move through five stages of light to deep sleep in recurring 90-minute periods,* but these cycles don't stop just because we're awake. The science shows that after working hard for more than 90 minutes, our brains begin to slow down to conserve energy. We become more reactive and less capable of thinking clearly and reflectively, or seeing the big picture. Our FAST thinking takes a firm grasp on the steering wheel, while our deeper SLOW thinking goes into hibernation. Psychologist K. Anders Ericsson, known for his research and theories on expertise, believes that we are designed to pulse, to move between spending and renewing energy, pointing out that top performers in fields ranging from music to science to sports tend to work in approximately 90-minute cycles, then take a break and start fresh.[33]

---

* Physiologist Nathaniel Kleitman introduced sleep cycles in his seminal 1939 book *Sleep and Wakefulness*. Kleitman introduced the concept of rapid eye movement (REM) in 1953.

These three Jumpstarting techniques can work wonders when it comes to ensuring that the Downgrading flaw
doesn't enter into your equation for winning the brain game.

---

**TAKEAWAY** ## The Flaw & The Fix

### DOWNGRADING

Downgrading is a futile attempt to declare victory through a
preemptive surrender. We downgrade our goals for several
reasons, including a natural tendency to sell our capacity
short, failing to construct goals with motive and means, and
a lack of good old-fashioned grit. A few simple techniques
for embracing possibility, constructing goals, and engineering fresh starts can help to jumpstart our mental machinery
and get us back on track toward solving our challenge.

PART THREE

# Mindless

## CHAPTER 6

# Not Invented Here (NIH)

*He who can no longer pause to wonder and stand rapt in awe, is as good as dead; his eyes are closed.*

**—ALBERT EINSTEIN**

Many years ago I played a dirty trick on a group of senior leaders inside a particular business unit of a fairly large organization that had hired me to help improve performance at a customer call center. Through my consulting work I had discovered that a group of about a dozen managers and supervisors of the command-and-control persuasion were causing some fairly serious issues. In one part of the operation, I discovered that a number of improvement suggestions by customer service representatives had simply never seen the light of day—ideas that would have made customers' lives easier and benefited the company. In another part of the operation, some extremely lucrative opportunities had been dismissed, each with what I considered a relatively high lost opportunity cost.

I presented my findings in a report that described how a number of managers (including some of the senior managers on the panel that had hired me) would not allow their subordinates to pursue ideas. They had various ways of shooting ideas down, many times dismissing them without consideration and, in one case, going so far as to have a no-suggestion policy.

The leadership panel took issue with my presentation. They argued vehemently that "that's not our culture," that "our people are our greatest asset," that "we value all ideas," and that I was way off-base. I held my tongue, realizing that the collective mindset was so deeply embedded in the culture that they could not see they were doing the very thing to me I was reporting on, right there and then. Luckily, an upcoming off-site presented me with the opportunity to demonstrate what I was talking about to them, because I got to design part of the agenda.

At the off-site, there were about 120 people of varying degrees of seniority and rank. We had a dozen table rounds, and I put an organizational cross-section of people at each. In other words, at any given table, there might be a management trainee or administrative assistant sitting next to a senior manager.

I gave the assignment, one of those widely available group priority exercises whereby you rank a list of items individually and then as a group and compare results . . . sort of a "wisdom of crowds" exercise to show that "we" is smarter than "me," that great ideas and solutions can come from anywhere, and are always better when developed collaboratively.

The specific exercise was called "Survival on the Moon," and the goal was to rank the 25 items with which you've crashed on the moon in relation to how important they were to your survival in making the 200-mile trek to the ship from which you've been separated in the crash. NASA had compiled the correct ranking, so there was actually a suggested "expert solution," but only I as the facilitator had it.

Except I *wasn't* the only one. I added a twist. At each table I put a ringer. I gave the lowest-ranking or most junior person the answer. When it came time to do the exercise as a group, I told them that it was their job to convince the highest-ranking and most senior people that they knew for certain what the right priority ranking was. They could say anything they wanted, short of telling the table that I had given them the NASA solution. I told them they could say that they had done the exact same exercise before at another company, or that they used to work at NASA, I didn't care. They just couldn't tell anyone our little secret.

During the group part, not a single table got the right ranking, *even though the best solution was in their hands.*

After debriefing the exercise in the regular way, which of course proved the point—but knowing the *Aha!* would be lost on the offenders—I had the ringers stand up. I announced that these individuals had the solution in their hands, because I had given it to them in advance.

I wish I had a camera to catch the red-faced managers. They terminated my contract shortly after that. But I had made my point, which was that Not Invented Here syndrome was alive and well, and wreaking havoc with the business.

## THE NIH FLAW

When advertising executive Alex Osborn introduced the world to brainstorming over a half century ago, he proposed four rules for applying one's imagination, half of which focused on preventing idea rejection: *defer judgment* and *build on others' ideas.* He was well aware of NIH before it was called NIH, and unfortunately, his rules have had little effect on our tendency to do just the opposite: *impose judgment* and *reject others' ideas*.

NIH is defined as a strong resistance to, or automatic rejection of, concepts—knowledge, ideas, solutions—produced somewhere else, somewhere external to the individual or team, often resulting in an unnecessary reinvention of the wheel. The pairing of these two aspects, external idea origination and immediate internal devaluation, is the defining characteristic of NIH.

Recall from the opening thought challenge that I clearly stated that previous solutions had included reminders, penalties, and incentives, none of which worked. Yet over a third of regularly proposed solutions are essentially some form of these: loyalty program, discontinue the shampoo, separate fee for shampoo, sell the shampoo at cost, "most wanted list" of offenders, shampoo in unmarked bottles, "do not remove shampoo" signs, free sample-size bottles.

The same is true of the videotape challenge. I believe that since I was an "outsider" to the teams trying to solve the challenges, my knowledge and solutions were rejected out of hand. So while the teams worked fairly well under Osborn's brainstorming rules, there was an unconscious and unspoken consensus that the rules did not apply to my ideas as stated in the challenge setup. There has been uncanny consistency over the years in my observations, and the result is always NIH and wheel reinvention.

History is littered with stories of initial NIH-type responses to new and novel ideas that eventually found success and have become so much a part of our collective experience that we can only marvel with glorious 20-20 hindsight at the apparent stupidity of the NIHers.

Take the case of the now ubiquitous hashtag (#). When Chris Messina, a former Google designer, conceived of a simple way to filter content and create channels on Twitter in 2007, he blogged about his idea:

> Every time someone uses a *channel tag* to mark a status, not only do we know something specific about that status, but others can *eavesdrop* on the context of it and then join in the channel and contribute as well. Rather than trying to ping-pong discussion between one or more individuals with daisy-chained @replies, using a simple #reply means that people not in the @reply queue will be able to follow along, as people do with Flickr or Delicious tags. Furthermore, topics that enter into existing channels will become visible to those who have previously joined in the discussion. And, perhaps best of all, anyone can choose to leave or remove topics that don't interest them.[34]

His idea was complete with syntax (rules) for how it would work, such as "No one owns or administers a tag channel," and "A channel is created the first time someone posts a status with a channel tag." He included Twitter page prototypes, as well as a test case focused on the popular SXSW conference. In other words, he had validated his concept through Prototesting. Twitter's reaction to his proposal? As Messina told the *Wall Street Journal* six years later, "[Twitter] told me flat out, 'These things are for nerds. They're never going to catch on.'"[35]

The hashtag was an external solution to an important user problem, which to Messina's way of thinking was how to enable Twitter users to "express more about the content they share in order to connect with more people."[36]

## NIH THROUGH THE YEARS

"Louis Pasteur's theory of germs is ridiculous fiction."
—Pierre Pachet, Professor of Physiology at Toulouse, 1872

"This 'telephone' has too many shortcomings to be seriously considered as a means of communication. The device is inherently of no value to us."
—Western Union internal memo, 1876

"Airplanes are interesting toys but of no military value."
—Marechal Ferdinand Foch, Professor of Strategy, Ecole Superieure de Guerre, 1904

"The wireless music box has no imaginable commercial value. Who would pay for a message sent to nobody in particular?"
—David Sarnoff's associates in response to his urgings for investment in the radio in the 1920s

"Who the hell wants to hear actors talk?"
—H. M. Warner, Warner Brothers, 1927

"The bomb will never go off. I speak as an expert in explosives."
—Admiral William Leahy, U.S. Atomic Bomb Project

"I have traveled the length and breadth of this country and talked with the best people, and I can assure you that data processing is a fad that won't last out the year."
—The editor in charge of business books for Prentice Hall, 1957

"He told me he didn't like their sound. Groups of guitars were on the way out."
—Brian Epstein referring to Decca Records executive Dick Rowe's rejection of The Beatles, 1962

"A cookie store is a bad idea. Besides, the market research reports say America likes crispy cookies, not soft and chewy cookies like you make."
—Response to Debbi Fields's idea of starting Mrs. Fields cookies

"There is no reason anyone would want a computer in their home."
—Ken Olson, president, chairman and founder of Digital Equipment Corp., 1977

"So then we went to Hewlett-Packard, and they said, 'Hey, we don't need you. You haven't got through college yet.' "
—Steve Jobs on his and Steve Wozniak's personal computer

While NIH in popular business literature is almost always discussed in a social context—organization, team, even a two-person partnership—it is my experience that it is entirely of an individual origin, perhaps a special strain of Fixation (see Chapter 2). I say this because over the course of the quarter century in which I've counseled senior leaders, I've seen hundreds of cases of NIH, even when a particular bit of external ingenuity is in the best interest of the larger organization. I've seen NIH play out under different situations and to several degrees, and it is not always directed toward concepts and knowledge developed outside a company. I've seen it happen inside teams, especially when the team members are geographically separated, and it doesn't seem to matter whether they are located on opposite ends of the campus or opposite ends of the earth. I've seen it happen, curiously, even when a senior leadership team spends millions of dollars on outside firms to conduct studies and offer objective recommendations: the information and ideas presented are perceived as less than brilliant, impractical, or not worth implementing, and so never are. One of the most prevalent strains of NIH, though, and perhaps the most deadly to a culture because of its power to stifle creativity and alienate people, is the kind related to pecking order, which is why I began this chapter the way I did.

Where there is some sort of real or perceived barrier—space, time, structure—across which concepts must travel, NIH can literally keep you out of the game.

## WHY NIH HAPPENS

Wikipedia offers a good starting point for understanding what drives NIH:

> In many cases, Not Invented Here occurs as a result of simple ignorance, as many companies simply never do the research to know whether a solution already exists. Also common, however, are deliberate cases where the organization's staff rejects a known solution because they don't take the time to understand it fully before rejecting it; because they would have to embrace new concepts in infrastructure or terminology; because they believe they can produce a superior product; or because they would not get as much credit for finding an existing solution as inventing a new one.

A study of the literature devoted to NIH reveals that it is above all a predisposition— acquired attitude or bias—arising out of perceived burden, mental load, or possible threat.[37] It lives in our FAST thinking more than our SLOW. Obviously, there are many rational reasons to reject any idea or solution. In fact, far more ideas should be rejected than accepted, because the ratio of good ideas to bad is hundreds if not thousands to one. Most people are familiar with the Linus Pauling quote: "The best way to have a good idea is to have a lot of ideas." Logical, rational rejection of ideas is a good thing, but, thankfully, it is not NIH.

NIH becomes more prevalent as we develop subject matter expertise, which is a form of power . . . "knowledge is power." Subject matter expertise is the mother of all biases. Chris and Dan Heath in their book *Made to Stick* referred to it as a curse, the "curse of knowledge." We saw in our discussion of Fixation (Chapter 2) how our brain patterns can prevent us from being able to see challenges in new or different ways. Special knowledge adds new wrinkles.

Psychologists maintain that deep but narrow bands of knowledge, aka *subject matter expertise*, provide us a bounded personal and social domain closely integrated with our self-image. As result, we perceive anything that may breach that domain as a potential threat to our status, position, or power base. This helps explain why NIH is so often discussed in the context of social groups and organizations.

NIH, then, is tied to domains of knowledge and activity we believe we own. If we're the expert, we should be the one with all the great ideas, or so the thinking goes. Irrational as it may be, if someone else gets an idea or conjures up a solution that lies within our domain of expertise, we somehow get a sense of diminished capacity: *I should have thought of that.* Fear then creeps in if we feel as though others may perceive us to be somehow less of an expert, especially if those others happen to be bosses, employers, or clients. That's when we double down on defensive maneuvers like NIH to protect our status, position, or power base.

## THE NEUROSCIENCE OF NIH

### Subject Matter Expertise & The Curse of Knowledge

Biology may play a part in Not Invented Here syndrome.

For one thing, we know from our discussions in earlier chapters that it is *attention density* that shapes and reshapes the patterns of connections in the brain by way of the quantum Zeno effect. Jeffrey Schwartz and David Rock, in their seminal article *The Neuroscience of Leadership*,[38] reveal that an individual with a deep and special expertise in one specific knowledge area has much different patterned thinking than someone with deep expertise in another area. In other words, since marketing specialists literally think differently than finance specialists, they will see the world quite differently.

Secondly, processing new concepts requires us to engage our SLOW thinking, which as you recall is lazy. New ideas and knowledge processing put a load on our prefrontal cortex, where SLOW thinking takes place. We are wired to preserve our resources, mental and otherwise, so we resist new ideas naturally and automatically, not because the ideas are bad, but because we would rather not expend the enormous energy it takes to focus dense attention and make new connections. The feeling is uncomfortable, so we avoid it.

Finally, Schwartz and Rock tell us that we do not receive the same chemical reward from other people's ideas as we do from our own. When we solve a problem ourselves, at the moment of insight around which new and complex

*(continued)*

connections are made, the brain releases an adrenaline-like rush of neurochemicals.

"These connections have the potential to enhance our mental resources and overcome the brain's resistance to change," write Schwartz and Rock. "For insights to be useful, they need to be generated from within, not given to individuals as conclusions. This is true for several reasons. First, people will experience the adrenaline-like rush of insight only if they go through the process of making connections themselves. The moment of insight is well known to be a positive and energizing experience. This rush of energy may be central to facilitating change: It helps fight against the internal (and external) forces trying to keep change from occurring, including the fear response."

In a counterintuitive way, then, coming up with our own ideas is cognitively easier than assimilating ideas of others, and more mentally rewarding.

If we take a step back from the neuroscience and psychology, and add a touch of Synthesis, it would seem reasonable to conclude that mental cost-benefit comparisons get made unconsciously when one is trying to absorb the ideas of others, and the perceived benefit erroneously ends up on the losing side of the cognitive scale. This is not an easy flaw to fix, given our neurological wiring. Like all of the previously discussed fixes, NIH requires us to flip the paradigm, engage our mind over our brain matter, and create the very connections that are so rewarding.

The best way to do this is to invoke the wisdom of Pablo Picasso, who famously said that "bad artists copy, great artists steal." Such a true anti-NIH approach enables you to look at how others have solved a problem, and thus avoid reinventing the wheel. Fixing the NIH flaw may just bring out the great artist in you!

## THE FIX: PROUDLY FOUND ELSEWHERE (PFE)

Had he suffered from NIH, Steve Jobs might never have even considered the pleas of Apple engineers Jef Raskin and Bill Atkinson to visit the Xerox Palo Alto Research Center (PARC) in 1979, much less be persuaded to do so. He might never have struck a deal with the Xerox venture capital division allowing it to buy 100,000 shares of Apple stock before it went public in exchange for allowing Jobs and his colleagues to get a good look inside PARC. He might never have persuaded Xerox scientist Larry Tesler to show him everything PARC was working on concerning computer user interaction. He might never have seen the graphical user interface PARC had developed, designed to look like a desktop, and converting traditional computer command lines and DOS prompts to icons of folders and documents that you could point to and click open by using something Xerox called a mouse. He might never have seen a new way to render characters on a computer screen, called bit-mapping, which enabled a stunning graphic display. He might not have seen a Xerox prototype computer called Alto running on an object-oriented programming language called Smalltalk. He might never have seen the future of computing, embraced Picasso's "great artists steal" notion, and taken the Xerox interface for Apple's use, boasting later that "we have always been shameless about stealing great ideas." He might never have dramatically improved on the concept, nor hired industrial design firm IDEO to redesign the Xerox three-button mouse to a one-button device. He might never have taken a team of Apple engineers and designers to a Xerox dealer to observe the Xerox Star, the first machine to feature the graphical user interface. He might never have hired Larry Tesler and Xerox hardware designer Bob Belleville to help Apple develop what would eventually become the first Macintosh computer.

And, in the second chapter of his career, after retaking the Apple helm after years of non-Jobsian leadership characterized by an acute case of NIH syndrome, Steve Jobs might never have brought in industrial designer Jonathan Ive to help him revitalize the company. And had Jonathan Ive suffered from NIH, he might never have "stolen" the design stylings and aesthetics of one Dieter Rams, genius designer of Braun fame.*

But Steve Jobs and Jonathan Ive were immune to NIH, as great artists are, and as a result achieved an unparalleled level of co-created product design that produced world-changing commercial elegance. They wore that immunity like a badge of honor, one that is now called *Proudly Found Elsewhere (PFE)*, a term coined at Procter & Gamble (P&G) in 2000, when P&G came under the leadership of A. G. Lafley.

The Jobs-Ive blend of creative execution and commercial value is rare. A. G. Lafley recognized as much when he

---

* There are many articles showing the uncanny resemblance between Braun and Apple products, including Gizmodo.com's *1960s Braun Products Hold the Secrets to Apple's Future* (2008) and Forbes.com's *Jony Ive's (No Longer So) Secret Design Weapon* (2013).

NOT INVENTED HERE (NIH) 143

evaluated the impact of P&G's innovation efforts. As Roger Martin tells the story, Lafley inherited a disastrous innovation effort that under previous leadership had tripled internal research and development investment but returned dismal results, with only 15 percent of innovation projects meeting sales and profit projections. Lafley knew more investment wasn't the answer, and began looking for a better way to innovate. As Martin explains it, Lafley "looked outside P&G to see how other organizations solved their innovation." He saw that it was the smaller entities that were more inventive, but it was the big companies that had the resources to develop and distribute innovations in ways the little guys couldn't. "Free of preconceptions about the 'right' way to innovate," Martin writes, "he set a target for P&G to obtain 50 percent of its innovations from outside the company by connecting with a wide array of outside innovators. P&G would then exploit its huge resource advantage to develop and commercialize the innovation. Lafley believed this strategy, dubbed 'Connect & Develop,' would enable P&G to parlay a relatively modest investment in innovation into above-average growth."

Yes, you read that right: fully *half* of P&G's new products must be originated from outside the company!

In a collective display of NIH, P&G's innovation staff resisted. But when you're the CEO of a multibillion-dollar global company, an executive edict is often all you need to banish NIH. Still, Lafley heard them out, realized they had assumed *Connect & Develop* was code for outsourcing, and quickly corrected their thinking by assuring them that the goal was to double or triple the commercial productivity of the innovation efforts. He then credited the top three innovation executives with formulating the initiative, two of whom—Larry Huston and Nabil Sakkab—wrote a popular article for the March 2006 issue of *Harvard Business Review*, in which they introduced the world to the term *Proudly Found Elsewhere*, writing,

> Lafley made it our goal to acquire 50% of our innovations outside the company. The strategy wasn't to replace the capabilities of our 7,500 researchers and support staff, but to better leverage them. Half of our new products, Lafley said, would come *from* our own labs, and half would come *through* them. It was, and still is, a radical idea. As we studied outside sources of innovation, we estimated that for every P&G researcher there were 200 scientists or engineers elsewhere in the world who were just as good—a total of perhaps 1.5 million people whose talents we could potentially use. But tapping into the creative thinking of inventors and others on the outside would require massive operational changes. We needed to move the company's attitude from resistance to innovations "not invented here" to enthusiasm for those "proudly found elsewhere." And we needed to change how we defined, and perceived, our R&D organization—from 7,500 people inside to 7,500 plus 1.5 million outside, with a permeable boundary between them.[39]

*Permeable boundary.* That is Synthesis (from Chapter 4 on Satisficing) at its finest.

What do you do if you don't happen to have the clout of an A. G. Lafley to mandate a company-wide permeable boundary? What do you do if you're essentially the CEO of You, Inc.? The two salient features of a PFE strategy are an outside-in flow of ideas, and an inside-out connection with sources of new (to you) ideas. I have found the following tools to be among the best ways to achieve both.

## Open Hackathons: Bringing the Outside In

Edmunds, a company with whom I've worked for over a half decade, is a family-owned business focused on using a blend of big data and the human touch to personalize and ease the car shopping experience for U.S. consumers. Each year since 2013, Edmunds has hosted an annual multiday innovation competition called Hackomotive, inviting individuals, teams, and even entrepreneurial companies to hunker down at their Santa Monica headquarters to create innovations that radically improve automotive retailing. Aside from the three cash awards given each year, a few winning ideas are invited to participate in an internal three-month-long accelerated development program, called Fastlane. Occasionally, these accelerators result in acquisitions, hirings, or a blend of both. It has become an enormously productive PFE effort, generating breakthrough ideas that create real customer value in ways the Edmunds-proper organization may never have considered.

Hackathons like Hackomotive have moved well beyond the technology-only focus that "hack" conjures up, to become a valid method of bringing a diverse and passionate group of people—designers, storytellers, marketers, coders, entrepreneurs—together over a short time to solve real-world problems and produce a basket of strong ideas. Innovation is a contact sport, and having dozens of talented individuals rub shoulders and put their heads together is bound to produce something profound.

Hackathons need not be open to the public; internal hackathons bring the same boundary-breaking enthusiasm and engagement that help to rid the culture of NIH.

## Knowledge Network: Reaching Out to Connect

During my tenure at University of Toyota, we encouraged individuals to engage fully with the outside, and to create what we termed a *Knowledge Network*, in much the same way P&G created a network of innovation partners with whom they could connect. Today, it's easier than ever to "connect and develop" with a wide variety of knowledge sources—you probably have dozens of ways in the palm of your hand, on your mobile device.

The goal of creating a knowledge network is much the same as A. G. Lafley's was in rethinking P&G's innovation framework: to become more productive and commercially valuable by exploring and exploiting the talents of others and bringing their ideas into your own repertoire through a more permeable boundary than you might have right now. This will help squelch any NIH-type tendencies you may entertain.*

One way to visualize a knowledge network is as a radar screen or target, segmented by categories of knowledge sources you find valuable and helpful.

---

* One of the things that has helped me squelch my own NIH is writing book reviews and conducting author interviews for the American Express OPEN Forum. Over four years and about 100 articles, I not only learned to appreciate the ideas of others, even if they conflicted with mine, I discovered that I truly enjoyed promoting them.

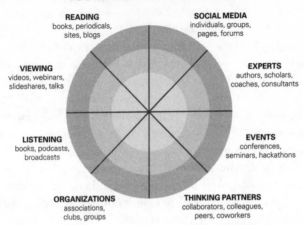

**YOUR KNOWLEDGE NETWORK**

To turn this visual into a useful tool, think about three possible levels of connections: the outer circle representing your loosest connections, and those in your innermost circle being your highest-quality connections. A high-quality connection is one that you reference and connect with constantly. The information, knowledge, and guidance you receive is excellent, and enables you to be faster, better, and smarter. The connection is also characterized by easy access. Your relationship to individuals is characterized by high levels of dialogue, responsiveness, and collaboration. Your high-quality connections enable you to get ahead.*

---

* In crafting a strategy for this book, I developed a project-based knowledge network. You have met some of my inner circle of THINKING PARTNERS throughout this book; individuals that I count on to mentor and advise me: Roger Martin, Jeffrey Schwartz, and Michael Schrage. Other cited individuals and works occupy the middle and outer rings.

To continuously improve the value of your knowledge network, focus on deepening ties to those with the potential to become part of your inner circle.

When I taught an experimental course on creativity and innovation for second-year MBA students at Pepperdine University in Malibu, California, I encouraged them to "connect and develop" through a knowledge network. Years later, I still receive notes from students telling me how their knowledge network has helped them to be more successful business professionals.

One of the best places to launch a knowledge network is at a hackathon. And if you're participating in a hackathon, don't give NIH a second thought. Your flaw is fixed.

---

**TAKEAWAY** The Flaw & The Fix

### NIH

When we perceive a boundary across which knowledge must travel, we resist and reject the ideas of others. Science tells us that assimilating the ideas of others drains our mental banks of cognitive resources without a corresponding reward. But by making a concerted effort to render our perceived boundaries more permeable by reaching beyond them to absorb concepts created and found elsewhere, we can improve our thinking and productivity.

## CHAPTER 7

# Self-Censoring

*Genius is not that you are smarter than everyone else.
It is that you are ready to receive the inspiration.*

**—ALBERT EINSTEIN**

If you had to come up with a list of ways to completely shut down a person's creative best, what would you put on the list? This is the central question behind one of my all-time favorite slideshows, by Harvard Business School innovation and strategy professor Youngme Moon, called *An Anti-Creativity Checklist: 11 Ways to Stifle Imagination, Innovation, and Out-of-the-Box Thinking (Guaranteed Results)*.[40] I like it for several reasons, not the least of which are that she used both humor as well as the "Opposite World" method (see Chapter 2) make her points. Here are my favorite five:

- **Play it safe: Listen to that inner voice**.
  What Moon is referring to here is the self-censoring voice in our head that whispers things such as *"Why would you go out on a limb to put your idea out there, what if people think it's stupid?"* Listening to such nonsense will most certainly stunt your creative output.

- **Know your limitations. Don't be afraid to pigeon-hole yourself.**
  This is that same self-censoring voice telling you quite clearly that you're not creative, not an innovator. It's putting you in a very confining, very false box.

- **Respect history. Always give the past the benefit of the doubt.**
  Moon is referring, again, to that overprotective voice that wants to squelch an idea even before it gets fully formed, warning your SLOW thinking not to bother getting engaged, and that you're better off going with what's worked in the past. It's far easier, safer, and more comfortable. Why waste valuable mental resources?

- **Keep your eyes closed. Your mind too.**
  Go ahead and play ostrich, implies Moon. All this change and disruption happening around us—new knowledge and new technology and ways of working—isn't going to last. They are just distractions and passing fads, so don't lean in, don't invest the mental energy to learn. In other words, stay right where you are. Your way of looking at the world is the only way. Sound familiar? It should, it's Fixation 101.

- **When all else fails, act like a grown-up.**
  Don't play, don't explore, don't ask why, don't rock the boat, just do your job, because there's real work that needs to be done.

All five are variations on a theme, which is the subject of the seventh and final fatal flaw: *Self-Censoring*.

## THE SELF-CENSORING FLAW

Not long after I began using the kinds of thought challenges I used with the LAPD bomb techs, I became aware that the elegant solution was present in the room during these types of sessions far more often than it was presented as *the* solution. In debriefing the exercise, I began asking how many people had thought of or discussed simply removing the shampoo bottle tops, or simply allowing videotapes to be rented unwound, even if they were not chosen as final ideas. Responses were of two varieties.

In the first, the solution, or one very close to the solution, was indeed suggested to the group, but did not make it to the top of the list—it was defeated by one of the other thinking flaws, in much the same way the solution to the Survival on the Moon exercise was: NIH.

In the second, an individual had thought of the solution, but did not raise it with the group. The first time this came to my attention, though, was not because someone raised their hand to say they had thought of the answer, but rather because an individual came up to me during a session break to tell me, rather sheepishly, that the solution had immediately popped into her head. I was keen to know why.

"Well," she began, "it just seemed easy and obvious, but I'm not very good at these kinds of things, so I figured my idea was too simple, and couldn't possibly be right."

This is classic Self-Censoring, which is the act of rejecting, denying, stifling, squelching, striking, silencing, and
otherwise putting *ideas of our own* to death. She had cen-
sored her thoughts before they ever saw the light of day. I
find this tragic. It's a crime of the mind. Ideacide.

Self-Censoring is perhaps the deadliest of the fatal flaws,
because any voluntary shutdown of the imagination is an act
of mindlessness, the long-term effects of which eventually
kill off our natural curiosity and creativity. Like NIH, it is
a special form of Fixation that borders on mental masochism: we field or create a great idea, we recognize it as such,
but deny or kill it anyway. Unlike NIH, there is no real or
perceived border or boundary to cross, other than our own
brain-mind barrier: the scrimmage line of the brain game.

As I mentioned in the Introduction, Self-Censoring is
rooted in a kind of personal fear that can not only silence
whatever creative instincts we may have, but also render
us mindless: exaggerating, catastrophizing, doomsdaying.
Welsh novelist Sarah Waters sums it up quite eloquently:
"Midway through writing a novel, I have regularly experienced moments of bowel-curdling terror, as I contemplate
the drivel on the screen before me and see beyond it, in quick
succession, the derisive reviews, the friends' embarrassment,
the failing career, the dwindling income, the repossessed
house, the divorce . . ."

There is no dearth of literature on Self-Censoring. It goes
by many names. A century ago, Carl Jung wrote that, "There
are, indeed, not a few people who are well aware that they
possess a sort of inner critic or judge who immediately com-
ments on everything they say or do."

My first formal introduction to this flaw came from Michael Ray and Rochelle Myers in their 1986 classic book, *Creativity in Business*, based on a popular course they co-taught at Stanford University Graduate Business School. In it, they introduce the Voice of Judgment, which their students fondly nicknamed VOJ:

> If you have trouble taking risks, or knowing when to take a risk, you are probably afraid of stumbling over the blocks thrown up by your own mind. If you lack the confidence to create, you are undoubtedly tuned in to the Voice of Judgment that all of us have within. You might think that the inhibiting pronouncements come from your associates, or the mores of your business environment, or society as a whole, but if you allow them to stop you, it's your own internal broadcast you're listening to.[41]

Ray and Myers acknowledge that judgment is "a wolf in sheep's clothing," and in general is a good thing that mostly keeps us on the right track, but that as we become more social animals and our desire to fit in and be accepted grows, "we submit ourselves to the kind of judgment that has conformity as its goal. This judgment condemns, criticizes, attaches blame, makes fun of, puts down, assigns guilt, passes sentence on, punishes, and buries anything that's the least bit unlike a mythical norm."

Novelist and screenwriter Steven Pressfield introduces us to the archenemy of creativity, which he names Resistance, writing in his 2002 book *The War of Art* that Resistance "is the most toxic force on the planet . . . the root of more unhappiness than poverty. . . . [Resistance] deforms our spirit. It stunts us and makes us less than we are and were born to be. Every sun casts a shadow, and genius's shadow is Resistance." In his 2011 follow-up *Do The Work*, Pressfield goes further, calling Resistance a "monster," an enemy in the form of "fear, self-doubt, procrastination, addiction, distraction, timidity, ego and narcissism, self-loathing, perfectionism, etc." He spends several pages giving Resistance a persona of its own: "Resistance will reason with you like a lawyer or jam a nine-millimeter in your face like a stickup man. . . . Resistance is not out to get you personally. It doesn't know who you are and doesn't care. Resistance is a force of nature. It acts objectively. Though it feels malevolent, Resistance in fact operates with the indifference of rain and transits the heavens by the same laws as stars. When we marshal our forces to combat Resistance, we must remember this. . . . Resistance is always lying and full of [expletive]."[42]

Jeffrey Schwartz, whom you met in Chapter 2, takes a less dramatic yet more cerebral approach, categorizing Self-Censoring thoughts among various "deceptive brain messages," which he defines as false, inaccurate, and unhelpful. Schwartz believes these thoughts take you away from what you truly want to achieve, and trigger what he calls our "Uh-oh" center, which sends out false alarms that something is wrong. Interestingly, the opening story of Schwartz's *You Are Not Your Brain* is quite literally dramatic, centering on Ed, a talented Broadway performer suffering from "intense stage fright and fear of rejection." Ed's brain was sending him messages telling him he was no good and undeserving of acclaim and success. "What's worse," writes Schwartz, "those deceptive brain messages about Ed were dead wrong." To the rest of the world, Ed (who sounds a lot like Henry Fonda, who threw up before he took the stage) was a beloved performer, a master of the stage, and could hold a crowd spellbound in their seats, often moving them to tears. But all Ed could think about was how terrible he was. "Rather than believing in his inherently wonderful qualities and impressive skills, Ed's brain was programmed to ignore his positive attributes and instead focus on what he might have done wrong or how people might perceive his mistakes—in essence, to home in on his minute flaws and imperfections."[43]

By any name—inner critic, VOJ, Resistance, deceptive brain messaging—Self-Censoring can snuff out our best thinking in a dash. If we let it, that is.

## WHY WE SELF-CENSOR

The causes of Self-Censoring are both biological and social, share the same origins and invoke the same brain functions as Fixation, and look a lot like NIH. So I will not dwell on them. There is a nuanced difference, though, and it is wrapped in the wisdom of the old idiom "once burned, twice shy." One touch of a red-hot stove is usually all we need to avoid that kind of discomfort in the future. The same is true as we experience the emotional sensation of stress from our first instances of social rejection or ridicule. We quickly learn to fear and thus automatically avoid potentially stressful situations of all kinds.

In the context of thinking and solving problems, the challenge is that our response to stress becomes so ingrained and so reflexive, so *mindless*, that our avoidance tactics automatically prevent new experiences that have potentially rewarding payoffs. When we self-censor, we don't even give these experiences a chance.

## THE NEUROSCIENCE OF SELF-CENSORING

### Uh-Oh, Oops, and the Threat-Protection System

What UCLA's Jeffrey Schwartz calls the "Uh-Oh" center,[44] Robert Reinhart and Geoffrey Woodman of Vanderbilt University call the "Oops!" response.[45] They are referring to the adrenalin-fueled threat-protection system in our brain that not only governs our fight-flight-surrender response but also enables us to learn from our mistakes.

Scientists have long believed that the origin of our threat-protection system is a bit of wiring in the brain: a jolt of negative electrical current generated in our frontal cortex when we make a mistake. Reinhart and Woodman showed in a recent study that our brain's mistake response could be controlled—increased or decreased—by intentionally zapping the brain with mild current. "We wanted to reach into your brain and causally control your inner critic," said Reinhart.

They gave subjects a "thinking cap": an elastic headband that secured two electrodes through which current was conducted by saline-soaked sponges to the cheek and the crown of the head. Participants got 20 minutes of gentle transcranial direct current stimulation in random directions: anodal (crown to cheek), cathodal (cheek to crown), or a placebo. A trial-and-error learning task followed, involving game control buttons corresponding to specific colors displayed on a monitor. Subjects had less than a second to respond correctly, making the activity error-prone and enabling brain activity to be measured at the very moment participants were making mistakes.

Results were intriguing. Under anodal current, the "oops!" spike of negative voltage was twice the usual level, and subjects made fewer mistakes and learned more quickly. Under cathodal current, the opposite results occurred: more errors and slower learning. The results highlight the importance of our inner critic, according to Reinhart: "So when we up-regulate [the 'oops!'] process, we can make you more cautious, less error-prone . . ."

But while this response is important to your ability to learn from mistakes, it also gives rise to self-criticism, because it is part of the threat-protection system. In other words, what keeps us safe can go too far, and keep us *too* safe. In fact, it can trigger Self-Censoring.

In fMRI studies, Paul Gilbert of Kingsway Hospital in the UK has shown that "the threat-protection mind is a self-critical mind," meaning our threat-protection system is stimulated even when there is no actual external threat, but just us being self-critical.[46]

If we are overly self-critical, according to Gilbert, we may attack ourselves, put others down, or seek some form of escape to "flee from the knowledge of our own faults."

Perhaps, then, it is this kind of mindlessness that is at the root of Self-Censoring. Mindlessness is not synonymous with stupidity or ignorance, nor is it in any way an indication of brain damage. As *Mindfulness* author Ellen Langer defined it for me: "When you're mindless, the past is over-determining the present. You're trapped in categories created in the past. You're trapped in a rigid perspective, oblivious to alternative perspectives. When you're mindless, you confuse the stability of your mindset with the stability of the underlying phenomenon. You think you know, then you find out you don't, because everything changes, everything looks different from different perspectives."[47]

I asked for a personal example. "I was at this horse event," she began, "and this man came up to me and asked me to watch his horse while he went to get a hot dog. He came back with the hot dog and gave it to the horse. And the horse ate it. And I said, OH MY GOD, what does it mean, 'horses don't eat meat'? And then I recognized that all information changes according to context, it changes over time, so every time you think you know, you're wrong.

"It turns out that we can find evidence for whatever hypothesis we entertain," she continued. "So if you ask about your thoughts . . . what's wrong with them, how bad they are, yours, mine, anyone's . . . you can easily find evidence. You can just as easily though find evidence for the opposite. And if you were more mindful, you'd probably do both. You have to recognize that events don't cause us stress. Stress is a function of outcomes, which are simply our interpretation of events, not of events themselves. When you're faced with something that seems stressful, you assume two things: first, that something is going to happen, and second, when it happens it's going to be dreadful." Both of which could be entirely false.

I interpreted what Ellen Langer told me to mean that since Self-Censoring is firmly rooted in the past, not the present, the messages arising from it can indeed be deceptive. And if what our censoring self thinks it knows may not be true, then automatically accepting it as some sort of inert truth is indeed mindless and self-defeating. Langer agrees: "When you think 'I know' and 'it is' you have the illusion of knowing, the illusion of certainty, and then you're mindless."

Allow me to share a personal example. In searching for new insights on the notion of mindlessness, I wanted to talk to Ellen Langer. Both her classic *Mindfulness* and deeply personal follow-up, *On Becoming An Artist,* are among my all-time favorite books. I didn't want to simply trade interview questions over e-mail, I wanted to talk to her about mindlessness as it relates specifically to Self-Censoring. The problem was, my own Self-Censoring was holding me back, triggered by the uncertainty of acceptance. It said, "Ellen Langer doesn't know me from Adam. She's a rock star, a heavyweight. She won't have time for me, and probably wouldn't talk to me even if she did. It won't happen." How did I know Ellen Langer had never heard of me? I really didn't. How did I know she wouldn't have time? I really didn't. How did I know she wouldn't talk to me? I really didn't. Had I mindlessly accepted these false Self-Censoring messages as gospel, I would have never had the pleasure of spending time with her.

Langer argues that we must learn to look at the world in a more conditional way, versus an absolute way, which was exactly the way the mindless me was approaching things at first. Understanding that the way we are looking at things is merely one among many different ways of looking at them requires us to embrace uncertainty. "Mindfulness follows from uncertainty. When you're uncertain, everything becomes interesting again," Langer told me.

That immediately brought to mind one of my fondest memories, involving my daughter when she was just a toddler of one: taking her with me on the short walk to check the mail. I live in a small enclave of homes in which all the mailboxes are together in a central location, less than a minute's walk from my front door—when I walk alone, that is. When I would take my daughter with me it was easily 20 minutes. Everything along the way, to and from, fascinated her: every pebble, ant, stick, leaf, blade of grass, and crack in the sidewalk was something to be picked up, looked at, tasted, smelled, and shaken. Everything was interesting to her. She knew nothing. I knew everything. She was mindful. I was mindless.

The trick to fixing Self-Censoring is making everything interesting again.

## THE FIX: SELF-DISTANCING

The opposite of mindlessness is of course mindfulness, of which there are two views, Eastern and Western. The Eastern view positions a specific method—meditation—as an essential component to achieving a mindful state. The Eastern view is more about quieting the mind, and suspending thought. This philosophy is almost the complete opposite of the Western view of mindfulness which centers on active thinking, not suspended thinking, as captured in Ellen

Langer's *Mindfulness*. Although a megatrend of Eastern mindfulness meditation is a rapidly growing one—a bright shiny new object in our Western business culture—it is not the view I wish to employ here in the context of solving difficult challenges that require us to actively think differently.

David Rock, in his book *Your Brain At Work*, defines mindfulness as "living in the present, being aware of experience as it occurs in real time, and accepting what you see."[48] Daniel Siegel of UCLA's Mindful Awareness Research Center agrees, defining mindfulness as "our ability to pause before we react," which in turn "gives us the space of mind in which we can consider various options and then choose the appropriate one."[49]

And as Ellen Langer tells us, "When we're mindful, noticing more things, it's literally and figuratively enlivening. You cultivate the ability to notice things around you. Noticing new things, in general, puts you in the present. Most important, it shows you that you didn't know that thing you thought you knew, which makes everything new to you again."[50]

It is this version of mindfulness—a higher-order attention, noticing moment-to-moment changes around you—on which the Self-Censoring fix rests. I call it Self-Distancing, which is apropos for several reasons.

First, the kind of heightened in-the-moment noticing at the core of mindfulness as we are defining brings to mind a classic concept well over a century and half old—*The Impartial Spectator*—first introduced by Scottish philosopher Adam Smith as a central figure in his 1759 book *The Theory of Moral Sentiments*, the precursor to his more well-known *The Wealth of Nations*. Smith wrote that we all have access to "the person within" by invoking "the impartial and well-informed spectator," which he defined as the ability to observe our behavior as an objective onlooker does, while remaining fully aware of our thoughts, emotions, and circumstances.

Jeffrey Schwartz uses the concept of the Impartial Spectator as an integral part of his therapy with OCD patients, teaching them to call on their "Wise Advocate" to assist them in reattributing their obsessions and compulsions as nothing more or less than deceptive brain messages. Schwartz and coauthor Rebecca Gladding describe the Wise Advocate as "The aspect of your attentive mind that can see the bigger picture, including your inherent worth, capabilities, and accomplishments. The Wise Advocate knows what you are thinking, can see the deceptive brain messages for what they are and where they came from."[51] Patients learn with great success to use the concept of Wise Advocate to view themselves as unbiased spectators and outside observers would.

Second, the modern term psychologists use for Smith's Impartial Spectator is in fact *self-distancing*, coined by researchers Ethan Kross and Ozlem Ayduk. What spurred Ethan Kross to investigate the concept in the first place was an act of mindlessness: he accidentally ran a red light. He scolded himself by saying out loud, "Ethan, you idiot!" Then he heard NBA superstar Lebron James in a 2010 ESPN interview following what many thought was an unthinkable and cold-hearted decision to leave his hometown Cleveland Cavaliers for the Miami Heat. James literally came under fire: fans were burning effigies of his jersey. Watching the videos during the interview, Lebron said, "One thing I didn't want to do was make an emotional decision. I wanted to do what's best for LeBron James and to do what makes LeBron James happy." The shift from first-person "I" to third-person "James" reminded Kross of his own switch after passing through the red light, and made him wonder if there might be something more to this quirk of speech, and if it might represent a method for changing one's perspective.

The short answer is yes, based on a series of studies by Kross and his team at the University of Michigan Self-Control and Emotion Laboratory.[52] In one study, they invoked stress and anxiety in one of the most powerful ways known to turn a challenge into a threat: public speaking in front of judges without sufficient time to prepare. In this case, college students had only five minutes to prepare and could not use notes. One group was told to use first-person pronouns to work through their stress; for example, "I shouldn't be so nervous," and "I will be fine." The other group was told to use their name or a third-person pronoun; for example, "Matt, don't be nervous," or "You'll do great." Not only did the judges find the latter group's performances to be more confident and persuasive, but the participants themselves reported far less shame and rumination than the first-person group. According to Kross, when you think of yourself as another person, it allows you to give yourself more objective, helpful feedback.

As Pamela Weintraub writes in the May 2015 issue of *Psychology Today:* "By toggling the way we address the self— first person or third—we flip a switch in the cerebral cortex, the center of thought, and another in the amygdala, the seat of fear, moving closer to or further from our sense of self and all its emotional intensity. Gaining psychological distance enables self-control, allowing us to think clearly, perform competently. The language switch also minimizes rumination, a handmaiden of anxiety and depression after we complete a task. Released from negative thoughts, we gain perspective, focus deeply, and plan for the future."[53]

## THE POWER OF SELF-DISTANCING

### Defying the Taliban

Perhaps you saw Malala Yousafzai hold Jon Stewart speechless on the *Daily Show* in 2013[54] as she talked about how at age 14 a Taliban soldier boarded her bus, pointed a gun at her head, and pulled the trigger. Listen to her toggle between "I" and "You":

> I started thinking about that, and I used to think that the Talib would come, and he would just kill me. But then I said, "If he comes, what would you do Malala?" then I would reply to myself, "Malala, just take a shoe and hit him." But then I said, "If you hit a Talib with your shoe, then there would be no difference between you and the Talib. You must not treat others with cruelty and that much harshly, you must fight others but through peace and through dialogue and through education." Then I said I will tell him how important education is and that "I even want education for your children as well." And I will tell him, "That's what I want to tell you, now do what you want."

Malala became the youngest winner of the Nobel Peace Prize at age 17 in 2014.

Experiencing Self-Distancing is not unlike the feeling you might get when you travel to a distant and unfamiliar place. As visitors we are *de facto* spectators: naturally mindful, fully present, noticing details the locals now take for granted. We are very much the outsiders, watching ourselves as we stumble and fumble local customs, chuckling at our folly rather than stressing over how stupid we are, as we surely would as natives to the land. And all the while we stay fully aware and alert to everything happening around us. We are in it, but not of it, so we are able to view ourselves in a more detached, rational, and objective way.

## THE FAR & AWAY EFFECT

### Distance Makes The Mind Grow Sharper

Ever wonder why other people's problems seem easier to solve than your own? It may be that you're simply too close to your own problems.

The "outsider effect" on creative problem solving has been studied, with intriguing and reinforcing results. Researchers at Indiana University wanted to explore how mentally distancing the imagination from the immediate context impacts creativity.[55] They gave two different groups of undergraduate psychology students a creative generation exercise which they termed a "linguistic skills task": list as many examples of "modes of transportation" as they could think of. There was no time limit, the instructions emphasized that there were no right or wrong answers, and responses could be "as commonplace or as creative and out of the ordinary as you like."

*(continued)*

Researchers randomly split the participants into two groups: "spatially distant" and "spatially near." The spatially distant group was told that the task was designed by students enrolled in an Indiana University–sponsored program called *Study Abroad Program in Greece*. The spatially near group was told that it was designed by local Indiana University, Indianapolis students.

This seemingly irrelevant twist made a world of difference: the group that was told the task originated in Greece generated significantly more, and more original, examples of transportation modes than did the group that was told the task originated nearby. "Furthermore," write the study authors, "relative to those who believed the generation task was from Indianapolis, participants exhibited greater cognitive flexibility when they believed that the task was from Greece."

The results underscore the power of Self-Distancing: those that imagined themselves in a distant and foreign land weren't limited by what they knew to be true of local transportation, and were free to list lorries, carriages, Vespas, and the like. Thinking about getting around Greece instead of simply Indianapolis opened their minds and invoked the outsider effect.

The researchers concluded that even minimal mental distancing oneself from the source of the problem can have a dramatically positive influence on creative performance.

When I asked Ellen Langer if she had a favorite tool or technique for managing mindlessness, her response involved a form of Self-Distancing. She reiterated that when you're facing something that's causing you stress, be aware that you've made two unwarranted assumptions: that something will happen, and when it does it will devastate you. Listen to her use of "you" and "yourself":

> So first say to yourself, give yourself three reasons, five reasons why this thing might not happen. It immediately becomes less stressful, because you just went from "it's going to happen" to "maybe it will happen, maybe it won't." Then ask yourself for three, five reasons why if it actually happens, it will be a good thing. Those reasons are easy to find once you ask the question. Now you've gone from "there's this terrible thing that's going to happen" to "there's this thing that may or may not happen, but if it does, it will have good things and bad things." That leads us to become less reactive to the world; you stay responsive, just not reactive.

As she relayed this simple method to me, I reflected back a few days to when I was immersed in my own Self-Censoring, which was causing me stress and rendering me mindless when it came to contemplating how I might possibly get to speak with Ellen Langer. I realized that I had worked through my dilemma in just this way, distancing myself from my Self-Censoring voice: "Wait a minute dude, you talked about mindfulness and mindlessness with your friend and mentor Roger Martin not long ago, and Ellen Langer's name came up. You should ask Roger if he knows her and might have spoken to her recently. And you should ask Karen Christensen too."

Karen Christensen is the editor in chief of *Rotman Management*, the journal of the University of Toronto's business school, of which Roger Martin is dean emeritus and faculty member, and to which I regularly contribute. It turns out I batted .500: Roger Martin didn't know her, but editor Karen Christensen did, and had in fact interviewed Ellen Langer in 2008 for the magazine. Not only did Karen e-mail me a copy of the interview, but she made the inquiry and introduction on my behalf. Ellen Langer responded within minutes to Karen, agreeing to chat with me, and two days later I was speaking to her, probing her thoughts on mindlessness, having just defeated my own. Had I not, you would be reading a decidedly different chapter on Self-Censoring.

Ellen Langer's final words to me may just hold the entire key to winning the brain game, so they will be mine to you: "As soon as you realize the issue looks different from a different perspective, take that perspective."

---

**TAKEAWAY**     The Flaw & The Fix

## SELF-CENSORING

The mental mechanisms by which we learn from our mistakes can and will automatically censor our present and future desire to explore and create, rendering and reinforcing a mindless state. By becoming more attentive to the moment and seeing the situation from the perspective of an objective outsider, this mindlessness yields to mindful thinking, a nonnegotiable requirement for winning the brain game.

# Solution to The Prisoner's Release

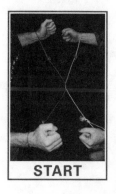

**START**

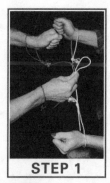

**STEP 1**

**STEP 2**

**STEP 3**

**FINISH**

# Solutions to Chapter 2 Insight Problems

1. An unemployed woman who did not have her driver's license with her failed to stop at a railroad crossing, then ignored a one-way traffic sign and traveled three blocks in the wrong direction down the one-way street. All this was observed by a nearby police officer, who was on duty, yet made no effort to issue the woman a ticket for violating the laws. Why?

   **SOLUTION:** The woman was a pedestrian.

2. A man leaves for a horsepacking trip on Sunday. He returns on Sunday, yet was gone for exactly 10 straight days, without crossing international date lines. How is this possible?

   **SOLUTION:** The horse's name is Sunday.

3. A young boy turned off the lights in his bedroom and managed to get into bed before the room was dark. If the bed is 10 feet from the light switch and the light bulb and he used no wires, strings, or other contraptions to turn off the light, how did he do it?

   **SOLUTION:** It was during the day.

**4.** Mr. Hardy was washing windows on a high-rise office building when he slipped and fell off a 60-foot ladder onto the concrete sidewalk below. Incredibly, he did not injure himself in any way. How is this possible?

**SOLUTION:** Mr. Hardy was on the first rung of the ladder.

**5.** Can you identify the pattern in the following letters?

A E F H I K L M N T V W X Y Z B C D G J O P Q R S U

**SOLUTION:** all letters in the alphabet made with only straight lines followed by those with curves.

**6.** Can you think of a word that forms a phrase with each of the following words: *shot*, *plate*, and *broken*?

**SOLUTION:** Glass

**7.** Move a single stick to correct the incorrect Roman numeral equation: ||| + ||| = |||

**SOLUTION:** ||| = ||| = |||

**8.** There are three switches outside a closed room. There are three lamps inside the room. You can flip the switches as much as you want while the door is closed, but then you must enter just once and determine which switch is connected to which lamp. How can you do it?

**SOLUTION:** Switch the first one on for a minute, then turn it off and turn the second one on. Enter the room and feel the two bulbs that are off. The warm one was turned on by the first switch, the light that is now on is connected to the second, and the other to the third.

9. A dealer in antique coins got an offer to buy a beautiful bronze coin. The coin had an emperor's head on one side and the date 544 BC stamped on the other. The dealer examined the coin, but instead of buying it, he called the police. Why?

   **SOLUTION:** In 544 BC, Christ would not be born for another 544 years, so "BC" would not have been stamped on an authentic coin.

10. Juliette and Jennifer were born on the same day of the same month of the same year to the same mother and the same father, yet they are not twins. How is that possible?

    **SOLUTION:** They are part of a set of triplets . . . or any sibling set more than twins.

11. Can you rearrange the letters n-e-w-d-o-o-r to make one word?

    **SOLUTION:** One word

12. A prisoner was attempting to escape from a tower. He found in his cell a rope that was only half the length needed to reach the ground safely. He divided the rope in half, tied the two parts together, and escaped. How could he have done this?

    **SOLUTION:** He divided the rope lengthwise.

**13.** A giant inverted steel pyramid is perfectly balanced on its point. Any movement of the pyramid will cause it to topple over. Underneath the point of the pyramid is a $100 bill. How could you remove the bill without disturbing the pyramid?

> **SOLUTION:** Tear, cut, or burn the bill.

**14.** In what direction is the bus pictured below facing, left or right?

> **SOLUTION:** Since no door is showing, the bus must be facing left.

**15.** Show how you can make the triangle below point downward by moving only three of the circles.

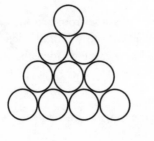
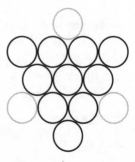

# NOTES

**Introduction**

1. *The Innovator's Hypothesis*, Michael Schrage. MIT Press, 2014.
2. "The Mashup: Merging Ideas Takes More Than Wishful Thinking, It Takes Integrative Thinking," by Roger Martin and Jennifer Riel, *Rotman Management*, Winter 2011.
3. Kross, E. et al, "Self-talk as a Regulatory Mechanism: How You Do It Matters," *Journal of Personality and Social Psychology,* Vol 106(2), Feb 2014, 304-324.

**Chapter 1**

4. *Blink*, Malcolm Gladwell. Little, Brown and Co., 2005.
5. San Wan Lee, John P. O'Doherty, Shinsuke Shimojo (2015), "Neural Computations Mediating One-Shot Learning in the Human Brain." *PLoS Biol* 13(4): e1002137. doi:10.1371/journal.pbio.1002137.
6. *A More Beautiful Question*, Warren Berger. Bloomsbury, 2014.
7. Interview for OPEN Forum, April 25, 2014. http://www.americanexpress.com/us/small-business/openforum/articles/the-power-of-asking-the-right-questions/.

**Chapter 2**

8. DeYoung C., Flanders J., Peterson J., "Cognitive Abilities Involved in Insight Problem Solving: An Individual Differences Model," *Creative Research Journal*, 20(3), 278–290, 2008.

**Chapter 3**

9. See http://marshmallowchallenge.com.
10. Bassett, Danielle and Grafton, Scott et al. "Learning-Induced Autonomy of Sensorimotor Systems." *Nature Neuroscience* 18, 744-751 (2015).

11. *The Design of Business*, by Roger L. Martin, p. 41. Harvard Business Press, 2009.
12. *Playing to Win*, by Roger Martin and A.G. Lafley. Harvard Business Review Press, 2013.
13. *The Innovator's Hypothesis*, by Michael Schrage. MIT Press, 2014.
14. Ibid.
15. Ibid.

### Chapter 4
16. "Doing Better but Feeling Worse," *Psychological Science,* February 2006, vol. 17 no. 2, 143-150.
17. "Maximizers, Satisficers, and Their Satisfaction with and Preferences for Reversible Versus Irreversible Decisions," *Social Psychological and Personality Science*, November 2015, vol. 6 no. 8, 896-903.
18. *The Sciences of the Artificial*, by Herbert Simon. MIT Press, 1969.
19. "The Mashup: Merging Ideas Takes More Than Wishful Thinking, It Takes Integrative Thinking," by Roger Martin and Jennifer Riel, *Rotman Management*, Winter 2011.
20. Adapted from "The Mashup: Merging Ideas Takes More Than Wishful Thinking, It Takes Integrative Thinking," by Roger Martin and Jennifer Riel, *Rotman Management*, Winter 2011.
21. Source of quote: Wikipedia.
22. "Integrative Thinking Three Ways: Creative Resolutions to Wicked Problems," Roger Martin and Jennifer Riel, *Rotman Management*, Spring 2012.
23. Both can be entered online.
24. "The Mashup: Merging Ideas Takes More Than Wishful Thinking, It Takes Integrative Thinking," by Roger Martin and Jennifer Riel, *Rotman Management*, Winter 2011.

### Chapter 5
25. *Cliffy: The Cliff Young Story*, by Julietta Jameson. The Text Publishing Company, 2013.
26. This story is adapted from *Playing to Win*, by Roger L. Martin and A. G. Lafley. Harvard Business Review Press, 2013.

27. *Meaning and Void: Inner Experience and the Incentive in People's Lives*, by Eric Klinger. University of Minnesota Press, 1977.

28. Brandstatter V., Herrmann M., and Schuler J., "The Struggle of Giving Up Personal Goals: Affective, Physiological, and Cognitive Consequences of an Action Crisis," *Personality and Social Psychology Bulletin* 39(12) 1668-1682.

29. Spunt R., Falk E., and Lieberman M., "Dissociable Neural Systems Support Retrieval of How and Why Action Knowledge." *Psychological Science* 21 (11) 1593-1598.

30. Duckworth A., Peterson C., "Grit: Perseverance and Passion for Long-Term Goals," Journal of Personality and Social Psychology, 2007. Vol. 92, No. 6, 1087-1101.

31. *The One Thing You Need To Know*, by Marcus Buckingham. Simon & Schuster, 2005.

32. Dai H., Milkman K., Riis J., "The Fresh Start Effect: Temporal Landmarks Motivate Aspirational Behavior," *Management Science*, June 2014 60:10, 2563-2582.

33. *The Cambridge Handbook of Expertise and Expert Performance*, edited by K. Anders Ericsson et al. Cambridge University Press, 2006.

## Chapter 6

34. http://factoryjoe.com/blog/2007/08/25/groups-for-twitter-or-a-proposal-for-twitter-tag-channels/.

35. http://blogs.wsj.com/digits/2013/10/03/how-twitters-hashtag-came-to-be/.

36. Ibid.

37. Antons D., Piller F., "Opening the Black Box of 'Not Invented Here': Attitudes, Decision Biases, and Behavioral Consequences," *Academy of Management Perspectives* 2015, Vol. 29, No. 2, 193–217.

38. "The Neuroscience of Leadership," Jeffrey Schwartz and David Rock, *Strategy+Business*, Issue 43.

39. "Connect and Develop, Inside Procter & Gamble's New Model for Innovation," *Harvard Business Review*, March 2006.

## Chapter 7

40. The original 2010 slideshow contained 14 items and can be viewed on Vimeo at https://vimeo.com/10175915. Five years after the original slideshow, Moon posted a revised checklist, containing three fewer elements. The 11-item version shown here can be seen on HBR at https://hbr.org/2015/04/an-anti-creativity -checklist-for-2015.

41. *Creativity in Business*, Michael Ray and Rochelle Myers. Doubleday, 1989.

42. *Do the Work*, Steven Pressfield. The Domino Project, 2011.

43. *You Are Not Your Brain*, Jeffrey Schwartz MD and Rebecca Gladding MD. Avery, 2011.

44. Ibid.

45. "Causal Control of Medial–Frontal Cortex Governs Electrophysiological and Behavioral Indices of Performance Monitoring and Learning," Reinhart R. and Woodman G., *The Journal of Neuroscience*, 19 March 2014, 34(12): 4214-4227.

46. Gilbert P. et al, "Having a Word with Yourself: Neural Correlates of Self-Criticism and Self-Reassurance," *NeuroImage* 49 (2010) 1849-1856.

47. My interview with Ellen Langer, October 5, 2015.

48. *Your Brain At Work*, David Rock. HarperCollins, 2009. p. 88.

49. Ibid, p. 89.

50. "Ellen Langer on the Value of Mindfulness in Business," by Art Kleiner, *Strategy+Business*, February 2015.

51. *You Are Not Your Brain*, Jeffrey Schwartz MD and Rebecca Gladding MD. Avery, 2011.

52. Kross, E. et al, "Self-Talk as a Regulatory Mechanism: How You Do It Matters," *Journal of Personality and Social Psychology*, Vol. 106(2), Feb 2014, 304–324.

53. "The Voice of Reason," by Pamela Weintraub, *Psychology Today*, May 2015.

54. Viewable on YouTube at https://youtu.be/gjGL6YY6oMs.

55. Jia L., Hirt E., Karpen S., "Lesson from a Faraway Land: The Effect of Spatial Distance on Creative Cognition," *Journal of Personality and Social Psychology* 96 (2009): 1047-61.

# INDEX

# ABOUT THE AUTHOR

**Matthew E. May** is an award-winning author and noted thought leader on strategy and innovation. A popular speaker, facilitator, and coach, he works with individuals and organizations all over the world.

Learn more at MatthewEMay.com